The 3 Pillars of Success for Funeral Directors

by Mark Bowser

Published by Bright House Publishers, LLC
3040 East 38th Street
Anderson, IN 46013

Distributed by IngramSpark

For ordering information, please contact Bright Corp. at 1-800-428-6424

Cover Design by BrightHouse Publishers, LLC

Library of Congress Publishing-in-Catalog

      Bowser, Mark.
              The 3 Pillars of Success for Funeral Directors
              ISBN: 978-0-692-16056-5 (paperback)

              1.   BUSINESS & ECONOMICS/General
              2.   BUSINESS & ECONOMICS/Leadership
              3.   BUSINESS & ECONOMICS/Sales & Selling

Printed in the United States of America

Table of Contents

Introduction

There are three fundamental pillars of success for your funeral home— and any organization, for that matter. Every funeral home that is succeeding is successful in these three pillars. Every funeral home that is failing is doing so because of a failure in one or more of these areas. This is true for any organization whether it is a nation, a Fortune 500 corporation, a nonprofit charity, a mom and pop small business, a church, a social club, a ball team—or your funeral home. Depending on the organization or group, they may call them by different terms and implement them a little differently, but when it comes down to it there are still three main pillars of success, and they are the subject of this book. The three pillars for your funeral home's success in their order of importance are:

Pillar One: LEADERSHIP
Pillar Two: SALES
Pillar Three: CUSTOMER SERVICE

That's it. Leadership, Sales, and Customer Service. That is the key to success. However, knowing the key and knowing how to use it to unlock the door aren't the same thing. Together, we are going to use the key to unlock the door to your funeral home's success. Together, we are going to take you and your organization to the next level. That is our goal. That is our purpose.

Before we jump into the subject at hand, you may wonder why I have the credibility to address this subject. Probably you have never heard of me. So, let me give you a brief summary of why you should trust me to be your guide on this journey.

I have been a Professional Speaker and Corporate Trainer since 1993. Since that time, I have successfully presented training seminars to hundreds of companies including Southwest Airlines, Dell Computers, Ford Motor Company, United States Marine Corps, Kings Daughters Medical Center, FedEx Logistics, Dallas Public Schools, Princeton University, Purdue University, NFL's Baltimore Ravens' Leadership Team, Department of Homeland Security, Honda, Indiana Chamber of Commerce, Makino Inc, Virginia Military Institute, Lockheed Martin, and many more. I have authored several books including *Sales Success* with the late Zig Ziglar; *Nehemiah on Leadership*; *Jesus, Take the Wheel*; and *Some Gave It All* with Danny Lane. For more details, visit my website at www.MarkBowser.com.

But the most important thing for you to know is that I grew up in the funeral industry and I am still involved in the funeral industry to this day. You see, my family is in its fourth generation of owning and operating the Bright Corporation in Anderson, Indiana. My granddad, William H. Bowser, purchased it in 1945 and we have run it ever since. Today, I am a Vice President at the Bright Corporation.

But that is enough about me. Let's get down to the business at hand—your funeral home's success.

Pillar 1: Leadership

Chapter One

The Keys to Empowered Leadership

WHAT IS LEADERSHIP?

Leadership can be defined as motivating one or more people to move in a certain direction. That move can be in the form of taking some action and/or acquiring a new belief. So, by this definition, leadership can also be defined as *Influence* and it also can be defined as *Sales*. Both are fundamental elements in your funeral home's success. You may have never thought of it that way. But the fact is, how good you are at influencing others has the greatest impact on your funeral home both internally and externally.

LEADERSHIP: THE ART OF INFLUENCING MOVEMENT TOWARD A VISION

Effective leadership is the most vital element in any organization. With it you can reach the stars. Without it the murkiest swamp will become your home. As John Maxwell said, "Everything rises and falls on leadership." So, what is effective leadership and how do we become that kind of leader? I believe one of the best definitions comes from author J. Oswald Sanders who described leadership as "Influence." Sound familiar? We all influence people every day. It may be as simple as influencing your co-workers on where to have lunch or as vital as influencing your teenager not to use drugs.

The first thing I think we need to understand is that there is a difference between an "Influential Leader" and a "Positional Leader." The Positional Leader has the title. I am the President. I am the Director. I am the King of the country. Well, that is great. But the title doesn't, in and of itself, make you influential. The Influential Leader may be the peasant of the kingdom or the entry level employee. Influence is about inspiring and moving people into action in order to reach a desired goal. I hope you have the position, but I also hope you have the trust, respect, and heart of your people. Whatever your position is at this time, I want to help you develop into the Influential Person that you were born to be.

Before we go any further, I believe it is important that we dig a little deeper into the explanations and actions of leadership. Let me ask you a question. Is there a difference between a leader and a manager? There is, isn't there? OK. What does a leader do? What is the first action that they take? They create a vision. They may not create a vision for the entire organization, but they definitely do for their part of it. All right, what does a manager do? They make it happen. They implement the vision. The leader creates where we are going and the manager breaks the vision into manageable parts and assigns the tasks to the right people and assures that it gets done. OK, let me throw another concept out there. What does a coach do? A coach motivates, inspires, teaches, provides resources, disciplines when necessary, etc.

So, which are you? A Leader, a Manager, or a Coach? The truth is that you are all three. I don't think we can separate it anymore. You have to be all three. You are a Leader/Manager/Coach. Now, that makes our task a little more daunting but will make you much more effective and successful in the long run. For the sake of simplicity, in most cases I am going to use the terms Leader and Leadership, but when I use those terms, I am talking about all three rolled into one.

Before we get into the nuts and bolts of leadership, let's pause for a moment and talk about three fundamental facts of leadership. Understanding these three facts will help jumpstart your development in becoming a more influential individual.

Three Facts of Leadership

1. One person can make a difference

2. You Need to start leading today

3. The office doesn't make the person

Fact #1: One Person Can Make a Difference

This saying is probably not new to you, but what pictures came to your mind when you read that statement? If you are like many people, it was pictures of Billy Graham, Martin Luther King, Jr, Mother Teresa, Ghandi, and many others. However, do you see someone missing from that list? I do. That someone is YOU!

Mother Teresa didn't go out to become a saint; she went out to save one dying person. She was walking down the street and saw a person dying in a gutter. She said to herself, "That is not right. Everyone should die with dignity." And the rest, as they say, is history. Great leaders, great physicians, sales champions, and consultants figure out how their influence can touch a life and by that action their influence may touch hundreds, thousands, and maybe even millions of lives.

So the question is where can your leadership grow to make a bigger impact than it does today? You are probably already making a difference, but how can your leadership grow? You make a difference and people need you!

Fact #2: You Need to Start Leading Today

Many times, young leaders for example will say, "I'm not ready to lead. I will wait till I read that leadership book, or go to that seminar, or learn that skill." Now, those are all important things and I encourage them, but the truth of the matter is that your funeral home and your team can't wait. You need to start leading today—and to learn as you lead. None of us will ever know all there is to leadership. It is a continual growing process. We can't wait until we know all there is to leadership or we will do absolutely nothing. We must become influential today and grow throughout our leadership journey.

Fact #3: The Office doesn't make the Person

Leadership is not about the corner office. Have you ever worked for someone who thought it was? They were more concerned with their promotion, their prestige, and their accolades. In the process, they lost their team (and many times their customers) as a result.

Now, please don't misunderstand me; I have no problem with comfortable offices and a comfortable work environment. In fact, I am for it. But we must not put the cart before the horse. Today, my family's company, the Bright Corporation, has a comfortable work environment and the executives have nice offices. But it wasn't always that way. My dad and my uncle made sure the horse came before the cart and now the company has the resources to support that type of environment. They were more concerned with helping their team succeed and serving their customers than they were about having a cushy sofa and a picture window in their office. As a result of this wise decision, they don't have a revolving door for their team or, worse yet, for their customers. Their team has tremendous loyalty. They have team members that have worked for the Bright Corporation for over twenty years. They have customers that also go that far back. How rare is that? Focus on your team and focus on your customers and the rest will take care of itself.

THE STYLES OF LEADERSHIP

There are three basic styles of leadership. An effective leader will use all three styles. Now, let me pause here for a minute and

The Three Leadership Styles

Autocratic

Democratic

Free Rein

say that I am not suggesting you change your style. What I am suggesting is that you become flexible with the styles. Would you agree with me that your style works some of the time and fails miserably some of the time? Why is that? Because one style doesn't fit every situation. What I am suggesting is that you use a more flexible situational leadership when it comes to the

Leadership Styles. Use the style that best fits the situation and the people involved.

Let me explain what each style is and when to use it.

Autocratic: The Autocratic Leader is more like a general, the commander of an army. He or she is a quick decision maker and tells others what to do. We saw this style a great deal in the corporate world in the 1950s through the 1980s. We still see it today, but not quite as much as in those earlier decades. Why did we see it so much in the past? Well, where did the CEOs and presidents of organizations get their training? Many of them came out of the military. Is autocratic leadership a good style for the military? Absolutely. Particularly in war time. Why? Because it was a time of crisis or emergency. Decisions had to be made and made quickly or people would die. Autocratic leaders took action and won wars.

After the war, those leaders came back and took their place in the corporate world. They discovered that their civilian counterparts didn't take orders like their military counterparts. This caused them some challenges. The leaders discovered that their style didn't work in every situation. They learned that they had to be flexible in their leadership styles. There is still a place for autocratic leadership in the corporate world because we have emergencies and other situations that require quick decisions and quick actions. But to maximize our effectiveness we must not get stuck in one style. Use the style that best fits the situation.

Democratic: The second style of leadership is the Democratic style. This is the leadership style of teamwork. It is run by democracy. We put things to a vote to make decisions and the majority rules. This is great for building team loyalty and participation, but let me ask you a question. Should every decision at your office be put to a vote? Of course not. So, when is this a good leadership style? Use it when you need to get buy-in from your team through open discussions, answering questions, and selling your vision, and when the decisions themselves aren't of major importance. Use this style to create rapport and teamwork.

Free Rein: In this style of leadership, we get out of the way and let our team do their thing. It is a style where there is definitely no micro-management. That is good. The challenge is that your team members have to be excellent, well trained, and go-getters for it to succeed. If you have a lot of entry level workers or workers who are new to the job, this is not the best style to be in. Those workers will need more of your input and guidance for at least the short term.

Well, there we have it. Three styles of leadership: autocratic, democratic, and free rein. They all have their pluses and they all have their minuses. Use the style that best fits the situation and the team members involved and you will find yourself succeeding in all leadership situations.

Chapter Two

The Influential Leader Empowers

"When you empower people, you're not influencing just them; you're influencing all the people they influence."

John C. Maxwell & Jim Dornan
Becoming a Person of Influence

WHAT EXACTLY is empowerment? It is a buzz word that we hear all the time, but what does it really mean? Well, the word "empowerment" can be defined as "to give the ability to." So, when we empower someone we are actually giving them the ability to do something.

The problem with empowerment is in how we give it to someone. We walk up to team member Jane and we say, "Jane, project ABC is now your baby. It is your project. Make it happen. Oh, by the way, if you need to make any changes, then come check with me first." Do you see what just happened? We just handcuffed Jane. We gave her the responsibility for project ABC but we didn't give her any authority. That is not empowerment.

Empowerment is actually an equation. It is not an equation original with me but one I have found to be very accurate and very powerful.

> ## Empowerment =
> ## Responsibility + Authority

That is true empowerment. We give Jane the ability to do project ABC by not only giving her responsibility but also the authority to make decisions and to make it happen. That not only empowers her but also begins developing her leadership skills. It also frees us up so that we can focus on the things that only we can do. We must never micro-manage people. When we empower Jane, it frees her and us to be our best. It also makes the team stronger. We become a leadership-focused team where we are developing everyone's leadership abilities.

You might be saying, "But what if Jane messes up?" Then use it as a teachable moment. We all mess up from time to time. When we learn from our mistakes, they actually make us stronger and draw us closer to our goal's completion.

Another point to remember is that we can't empower every team member the same way. Why? Because not everyone has the same experience or gifts. If we over-empower someone they get over their head and they begin to drown. I have seen this happen and it is devastating for the team member and the team. Everyone is an individual and we must lead them to success at their own pace. Help each member on your team be the best they can be — and your success (and theirs) is secure.

So, how do we do this? Well, let's start with the qualifications to empower someone. There are four qualifications that I believe must be present in order to effectively empower someone.

One, **position**. Fred Smith said, "Who can give permission for another to succeed? A person in authority. Others can encourage, but permission comes only from an authority figure: a parent, boss, or pastor." Mr. Smith is right. Are you in a position of authority with this person you seek to empower? If not, you can't empower them. You can motivate and inspire them, but not empower them. You must have the position to truly empower someone.

Two, **relationship**. You must have some sort of a relationship with them. If they have very little contact with you, then you won't be able to effectively empower them. Even if you are their boss, you can't empower someone unless you have a working relationship with them.

Three, **respect**. There has to be mutual respect for the empowering relationship to be truly effective.

Four, **commitment**. There needs to be a commitment on your part as a leader. You are in it for the long haul. You don't give a team member their assignment and then disappear to another project. As a leader, you need to be available—available for guidance, available for strength, and available for help. On the other hand, the team member needs to be committed to you as their leader and to the organization to do the very best job they can—committed to go the extra mile, to give that extra amount.

Those are the four qualifications to empower someone. Once they are in place, we can move to the empowering process itself. There are also four keys to empowering people.

How to Empower People

1. Discover their strengths

2. Develop their strengths

3. Give them a project

4. Help them succeed

First, you have to discover their strengths by observing them. Second, like a great coach, you must help them develop their strengths. Their strength is like a muscle. Without use, it gets weak. With constant use, it grows strong and powerful.

The third thing you must do to empower them is to give them a place to use their influence. A basketball player might have a sweet jump shot but it doesn't really do any good until the coach puts him in the game. We must put our team member in the game. Once they are in the game, we move to the fourth key, which is to help them succeed. Chances are they will make some errors. Not a big deal. Coach them to success. Even LeBron James needs a coach. We all do. A great coach can pull out the best from their team members.

So, do you sometimes feel overwhelmed at work? Too much to do and not enough hands to do it? Or is it you haven't empowered those hands to do it? Take a good look at your winning team and start empowering them—today.

Chapter Three

Connecting & Building Rapport as a Leader

BUILDING TRUST and rapport with your team is of utmost importance for any leader. United States President Abraham Lincoln spent 75 percent of his time meeting with people. Lincoln believed that a leader must stay close to people. Leaders are other-oriented. Lincoln knew that others were a great source of information. Lincoln also understood that his people were the team's greatest asset. His philosophy was to see as many people as he could.

Since rapport is such a vital element, how do we connect with people? In a later section in this book, we are going to lean on Dale Carnegie to teach us how to connect with most everyone in our lives. At this point, I believe it is important for us to take a look at rapport from a leader's standpoint.

There are four things that I believe are important for us to keep in mind if we are going to build rapport as a leader. One, **Get out among the people**. In his fabulous book *Lincoln on Leadership,* Donald T. Phillips said, "Lincoln even went to the field to observe or take charge of several battle situations himself, coming under fire at least once (one of the few American presidents to do so while in office)." Leaders have to be available to their team members. One of the problems is that in many cases, there is a separation between the leader and the team. I call this the "Ivory Tower Syndrome." The leader appears to live in an Ivory Tower and be unreachable to the team. This creates division, lack of trust, and eventually failure. Leaders must be available.

One of the best ways to get out among your people is to follow the strategy of "Leadership by Walking Around." You literally walk around. You are present, seen, and available. For example, you come in the office in the morning and you walk out among your team. You come up to Fred and say, "Good morning, Fred. I heard that your son Jim had a baseball game yesterday. How did he do?" Do you think this connects with Fred? You bet it does. You do the same thing with others on your team. I am not saying you have to spend five minutes with each team member. Make it informal. Just go out and talk with them.

I know what you are thinking. "Mark, I don't have time to do that. I am busy." Let me say this, you don't have time *not* to lead by walking around. Leaders who have bought into this philosophy of being present include Zig Ziglar, General Norman Schwarzkopf, and Lee Cockerell of Disney fame. The connected team is a more productive team.

The second strategy is to **get the facts**. As the leader, you have to make sure you are up-to-date and accurate on the important details of your team and organization. If you're not doing this, you will lose credibility in the eyes of your team, and that is the first step to failure.

Third, you need to **have an open door philosophy**. This means you are approachable. Let me give you a couple of examples from people who have attended my business seminars. One gentleman made a one-on-one appointment with each and every one of his team members. This was their individual time with their leader. They could talk with him about anything. It was their agenda, not his.

Another gentleman had an equally effective approach but with a little twist. Instead of setting an appointment with each team member, he had open office hours. He told his team that he would be in his office at a certain time, and anyone who wanted to speak with him during that time could. He disciplined himself and made sure that he was in his office at the appointed times.

Having an open door philosophy breaks down the walls of the Ivory Tower. We become approachable, reachable, and connected with our teams.

Fourth, **return favors before favors are due**. Now, what does this mean? It means one simple word—networking. We have to network with people. Networking has become popular, but is it really that important? Harvey Mackay wrote a book a number of years ago titled *Dig Your Well Before You're Thirsty*. It is advertised as the only networking book you will ever need. It is a fantastic book. And Charlie "Tremendous" Jones said, "You are today what you'll be five years from now, except for the people you meet and the books you read." So, yes, networking and connecting with people is extremely important.

How do we network with people? Well, let's go back to our principle of **returning favors before favors are due**. This is written in a very specific way for a very important reason. You see, many people network and connect with people in order to gain something. It's the old concept of "what's in it for me?" This is the *wrong* motive to network and connect. The *right* motive is to give. How can I be an asset to that person? How can I help them reach their goals? By doing this, you help other people—and guess what? The icing on the cake is that you are helping yourself, too. Can you throw a beach ball into the ocean without it coming back to you? As my co-author of *Sales Success,* the late Zig Ziglar said, "You can have everything in life that you want as long as you help enough other people get what they want." My friend, make this the cornerstone of your networking and rapport and you will have all the friends, love, and success you will ever want.

Please network with me at www.Linkedin.com/in/markbowser or email me at mark@BrightCorporation.com. You can also connect with me at my personal website which is http://www.MarkBowser.com.

Chapter Four

The Influential Leader Believes in People

"Help people believe in themselves by believing in them first."
Mark Bowser

"When you believe in people, they do the impossible."
Nancy Dornan

A LEADER believes in people. Even when we don't see them at their best, it is important to believe the best about them. It has been said to see people not as they are but as they can become. By doing this, we help them become that person. President Abraham Lincoln pardoned many people who deserted during the American Civil War. He said, "If Almighty God gives a man a cowardly pair of legs, how can he help their running away with him?" You see, Lincoln led with kindness. This is not a weakness, but a great strength.

Lincoln even set an excellent example for his own two sons, Willie and Tad. Unaware of their father's kindness toward negligent soldiers, they one day learned a lesson from the President they could not easily forget. As the boys enjoyed playing with toy soldiers, one of their toy soldiers got in trouble and was going to be punished severely. Lincoln, overhearing his sons' play, wrote on Executive Mansion stationery:

The doll Jack is pardoned. By order of the President.
A. Lincoln.

Kindness creates trust, openness, and creativity for a team both with each other and with their leader.

One way to see your people as they can become is to go through what I call a Strengths Inventory. The idea is to focus on their strengths, not their weaknesses. At this time, I want you to think of four people that you lead. What are their strengths? What are they good at? Write this down in the space below. Remember, don't write down weaknesses, just strengths.

_____ (Name) **Strengths:**

_____ (Name) **Strengths:**

_____ (Name) **Strengths:**

_____ (Name) **Strengths:**

Chapter Five

The Influential Leader Enlarges People

"See the person you want to mentor as they can become, not as they currently are."
Mark Bowser
Some Gave It All

"Mentoring is pouring your life into other people and helping them reach their potential."
John C. Maxwell & Jim Dornan
Becoming a Person of Influence

"Lead them step by step to the person they can become."
Mark Bowser

ONCE YOU KNOW an individual's strengths, the next step is to enlarge them. Enlarging people is mentoring them. There are four steps to the successful enlarging process.

HOW TO ENLARGE PEOPLE

One, give them access to a training library. A training library includes personal development books, audio, video, and DVD programs. Encourage your team to become readers. Research shows that if we commit to reading one book a month in whatever area we choose to develop ourselves in, that in five years, we will be in the top 5 percent of experts in that area in the world. That is powerful, but it also shows how few people take action on this. So, what kind of time commitment are we talking about for the average reader to read one book a month? About 15 to 30 minutes a day. That's it. A small discipline that can lead to your success. Amazon.com is a great resource for finding the books you want to read. You can even visit my author page at www.Amazon.com/author/markbowser.

Research also shows the value of listening to audio programs. For example, I think it was the University of Southern California who discovered that if we live in a metropolitan area, we could gain knowledge equivalent to a college associates program in three short years just by listening to audio programs during our commute to and from work. Incredible! Audible (an Amazon company) is a great resource for audiobooks and audio programs. Another great resource is Made for Success which is owned by a friend of mine, Bryan Heathman. You can visit their website at http://www.MadeForSuccess.com.

Two, open them up to growing experiences. A growing experience can be just about anything. It can be serving on a committee, joining a project team, or attending a training seminar. Growing experiences not only help us improve, they help motivate us, too.

Three, challenge them to success. This means stretching your team member outside their comfort zone. There is no real growth without stretching. Just like an athlete who stretches before competition, stretching outside our comfort zone prepares us for future and greater success. One caution: don't overstretch your team member. In other words, stretch them outside their comfort zone but not too far outside their comfort zone. Just as a baby doesn't go from crawling to running, they must walk before they run.

Four, set them up to succeed. Remember, success breeds more success! Our job as leaders is to provide our team members with everything they need to succeed. If that is training, then give them training. If that is resources, then give them resources. If that is help and support, then give them help and support.

Believing in and enlarging your team members is a prerequisite for your team's success. Do this and you are virtually guaranteed success.

Chapter Six

A Practice of Integrity

*"Hold onto wisdom and integrity as if it were your
very life—because it is!"*
Mark Bowser
Jesus, Take the Wheel

WHAT do you think: Should managers and supervisors teach
right from wrong? Let me ask you another question. What do
you think of Enron, WorldCom, and the other companies that are
in deep trouble or have crumbled because of unethical behavior?
Should managers and supervisors teach their employees (the
future managers and leaders) right from wrong? *YES! YES! YES!*
If we and our businesses are going to thrive, we must adopt into
our lives and teach into other peoples' lives the attitude that
character does mean something.

It is interesting that this topic has become a national debate.
This is good. Even though it doesn't appear that character wins
all the time—*TRUST ME; CHARACTER ALWAYS WINS IN
THE END.*

For the next few minutes, let me guide you on a journey to
three values we must teach our teams and explore how we can
motivate them to live those values.

The first value we must teach our teams is the value of
integrity. One motivational speaker used to define integrity as

wholeness. In his view, as long as you are whole or congruent to your values then you have integrity. Well, he is half right. What if you have the value that it is fine to murder people? If you are whole and congruent to that value then according to his definition we can murder and still have integrity. That is why a half-truth can mess your life up. He is right that integrity is wholeness. But the dictionary doesn't stop there. It tells us exactly what to be whole *to*. It talks about adhering to honesty and morals, being whole to those values. That is the integrity we *must* live and teach.

The second value we need to impart to our teams is that of **leadership.** Yes, true leadership is a value. So, what is leadership? Remember J. Oswald Sanders's definition? He defined leadership with one word: Influence. Leaders are able to influence people to take action. I believe true leadership is "morality influence." We need to motivate people to put morality and ethical goals into action.

The third value we need to express is that **Means Matter.** The results-at-any-cost mindset is dangerous and wrong. It is what has gotten companies in such deep water. If we want to have true success then we must be results-minded but with ethics leading the way.

All right, there you are, three values—Integrity, Leadership, and Means Matter. Now, how do you get your team to grab hold of them? I believe there are three ways to do that. One, you must **live them.** You set the tone. You are the example. You are the model. Two, **teach them and preach them.** You have to be the voice of right. U.S. President Theodore Roosevelt spoke of using his bully pulpit. You must use your bully pulpit to positively teach right from wrong. Third, **expect them.** Don't settle for anything less. Keep your standards high. Expect the best!

Chapter Seven

The Leader's Tool Chest of Credibility

IN ORDER TO BE successful, a leader must have credibility. In fact, unless you have credibility in the eyes of your team members, they won't follow you. So, in this chapter, we are going to discuss the four tools in the Leader's Tool Chest of Credibility. I want you to think about your tool chest at your funeral home or at your house. Go out to the garage or wherever you keep it. Open it up. What do you see? I can almost guarantee that you will see at least two tools. Can you name them? That's right. A hammer and a screwdriver. In my opinion, you don't have a tool chest unless you at least have a hammer and a screwdriver. These are the basics and some of the most important tools. Just like your tool chest, a leader must have a hammer and a screwdriver. These basic tools together make up the first tool in our tool chest of credibility and it is called **Lead by Example.**

TOOL # 1: HAMMER/SCREWDRIVER (LEAD BY EXAMPLE)

A number of years ago, I worked on the production staff of Peter Lowe International. They are the organization that put on the large *SUCCESS* seminars (today they are called *Get Motivated!* seminars). They are the largest business seminars in the world. One of my main responsibilities was to work with the resource products (books, videos, and audio programs) for the events. I remember a very busy seminar. I think we were in Denver. We had a lot of people wanting to invest in the resources, so many that we had too many customers. Now, this is a good thing but it is still a challenge to service them effectively.

During the seminar, Peter Lowe's number two guy came up to me and asked, "Mark, how can I help?" I said, "I need people." What I meant was that I needed him to transfer some people from the other teams to my team for the short term. What he did was even more impressive.

He jumped behind the table and started serving customers himself. He figuratively rolled up his sleeves and jumped on the front lines with his team. That made an impact on me. He showed me that day that he wasn't going to ask me to do anything he wasn't willing to do himself. He led by example. That day, his credibility went way up in my eyes.

Tool #2: The Power Saw (Words Mean Something)

I think many times, we as leaders use our words too casually. Words mean something. Communication can be one of our greatest dreams come true or our worst nightmare. Has anything like this ever happened at your office?

Team member: "Can I have Friday off? I need to take care of _____."

You: "Sure, not a problem."

Thursday rolls around and the circumstances change and you go up to your team member and say, "Sorry, you can't have Friday off now."

By doing this, what have you taught your team member about you and your word? That you can't be trusted.

Now, I understand that sometimes circumstances do change, but all I am really saying is be careful how you use your words. There is nothing casual about effective communication. Relaxed, yes. Casual, no. Words Mean Something and we have to do our best to always be truthful, accurate, kind, courteous, and clear.

TOOL #3: THE TAPE MEASURE (COMMUNICATE THE VISION & MISSION STATEMENTS)

Why does your funeral home exist? Where are you going? How do you plan on getting there? Not always easy questions. But they are some of the most important questions that you can answer for your team. Those answers will make a world of difference not only in your leadership credibility but also in your results.

TOOL #4: THE GLUE (BEFORE YOU DELEGATE, DO SOME OF THE UGLY TASKS YOURSELF)

If all you do is delegate the ugly stuff to your team and keep the nice, clean tasks for yourself, your credibility will drop like a muddy brick in a pond. My best advice is to do some of the ugly tasks yourself. Delegate some of the clean tasks. Why? Well, your credibility will go up in the eyes of your team. You see, the time will come when you will need more help, and then when you delegate those ugly tasks, your team will jump in and pick up the ball. Why? Because they know it isn't that you are unwilling to do the ugly tasks (because they have seen you do them), it is that the team is in crunch time and you need their help.

Well, there you have it. Four tools to greater credibility. One, The Hammer/Screwdriver, Two, The Power Saw, Three, The Tape Measure, Four, The Glue. Use these four tools regularly and before you know it your team will trust you more, believe in you more, and follow you more.

Chapter Eight

THE LEADERSHIP SUCCESS TRIANGLE

WHAT IS IT that makes some leaders more successful than others? I call it the Leadership Success Triangle. It is not original with me. In fact, I am not positive who came up with this concept. It just keeps getting passed down...because it works!

So, how does a triangle help us to be more influential? Take a look at the diagram below.

Let me explain how this works. At the top of the triangle, we have vision. Vision is vital. Vision is critical to your organization's success. King Solomon said, "Where there is no vision, the people perish." In other words, where there is no vision, your team fails. Where there is no vision, your team walks around in chaos. As we asked earlier, where is your funeral home headed? What is your Vision Statement or Purpose Statement? These are big questions but also very important ones to have answered.

Another key to vision is to have a challenging vision. I think that many times we sell ourselves short. Our vision is to walk around the block rather than walk around the world. We need a challenging vision not only for ourselves but also to infuse passion and enthusiasm into our team. A challenging vision doesn't mean we know how to reach it today. A challenging vision is one we believe is worthwhile and possible.

A leader I think about when it comes to having a challenging vision is President John F. Kennedy. In 1961, President Kennedy stood before the world and announced it was America's goal before the decade was out to land a man on the moon and return him safely to earth. That's a big vision. That wouldn't be a simple task for NASA today. But think about it. What was going on in 1961 when President Kennedy made that statement? The United States was getting clobbered by the Soviet Union in the space race. The U.S. had rocket after rocket blow up in their faces. Then, in 1961, the U.S. managed to have a victory. We launched Alan Shepard into space and we got him home without killing him. Shortly after that victory is when President Kennedy stated his goal.

If you were one of the scientists in 1961 hearing the President make such a statement, what do you think your reaction would be? "We are going *where*? Are you kidding? Man, we just barely got the guy up there and now you want to go to the moon?" But what happened a few short years later? It was July 20, 1969 when Neil Armstrong and Buzz Aldrin stepped off the *Eagle* lander and became the first people to walk on the moon. And of course, we got them home safely.

A challenging vision doesn't mean you know how to do it today. But it is one that is worthwhile and possible, and one which will stretch you and your team. That is a worthy vision. One worth pursuing.

In the middle of the triangle is where we find your people, your team. Take a look at the diagram now.

VISION

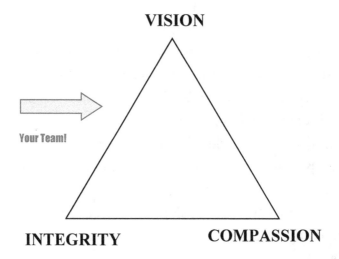

Your Team!

INTEGRITY   **COMPASSION**

This is where many leaders get messed up. Many leaders feel it is their job to get their ship (their organization) to move. That they are the motor of the ship. We, as leaders, are not the motor of the ship. So who is the motor? Your team is the motor. What are we? We are that little piece in the back of the ship. We are the rudder. We steer. We guide. We direct the team toward the vision.

Now, the next question is how do we get our team (the motor) to move toward our vision? That is where the base of the triangle comes in. The base is all about us as leaders. In order to get the team to want to move towards the vision, we need to be leaders of integrity and compassion.

Let's take a look at each side individually. First, let's look at integrity. Why is it important to get your team to move toward your vision? Not only because it is the right thing but also because it is the effective thing. Your team is asking themselves questions like, "Can I trust her? Can I trust him? Can I trust my leader?" Think just for a moment about a leader you don't trust. Do you care where they are going? Do you want to go with them? I doubt it. If we haven't earned our team's trust, then they most likely won't jump on the bandwagon to reach the organization's goal. This is where I believe we can learn from President Kennedy's faults as well as his successes. President Kennedy was a very visionary leader but he wasn't a very integrity-oriented leader. It is my belief that if we knew then what we know now about President Kennedy's lack of integrity, not near as many people would have jumped onto his bandwagon. Why? Because they wouldn't have trusted him. People will follow a leader they trust even if they don't understand everything. People will rebel against a leader they don't trust no matter what the goal is.

The other side of the triangle's base is compassion. We need to be compassionate leaders. This is frequently defined as the "servant leader." Let me ask you a question. Have you ever worked for someone who wasn't compassionate? Who were they concerned about? Themselves. They would say or believe concepts such as, "Your job is to make me look good. Your job is to help me get my promotion." Well, do you trust that kind of leader? Do you care where they are going? I doubt it.

A compassionate leader looks at it differently. They look at this way: "How can I help this person succeed? How can I help my team win? How can I get them all the resources they need to do their jobs more effectively?" You see, it is a paradox. When we help them, they help us. Remember what Zig Ziglar said: "You can have everything in life you want, if you will just help enough other people get what they want." And when they know that we have their best interests in mind and they trust us, guess what happens? They run towards our vision. Why? Because they want to reach it as bad as we do. This is why some leaders are more effective than others. They understand how to motivate others. They live by the Leadership Success Triangle and they and their teams are champions.

So, grab hold and take action on this concept and before you know it, your ship will be steaming towards your vision of a brighter tomorrow.

Chapter Nine

Succeeding Through Power Communicating

IN MY BOOK *Unlocking the Champion Within*, I delve into the topic of effective communication. That is because our success and failure rests on how effectively you and I communicate. We cannot "influence" as leaders if we cannot communicate effectively. Because it is so important, I have decided to include that chapter in this book too. Grab hold of effective communication and you grab hold of your future.

It has been said that public speaking is a fear worse than death for many people. Well, the truth is that we will not be as successful as we could be unless we improve our communication skills. In this chapter, we are going to explore some insights and action steps which lead to more effective communication. The only way to really conquer a fear is to confront it and jump right in. With that in mind, let's get started.

1. Realize that communication may be the most important skill we can learn. We all need to be able to express our thoughts effectively. We are creatures of relationships. Relationships are very important to us. In order to make our relationships better we must make our communication better.

2. Guard our tongues. Sometimes the most important message is the one we never give. Have you ever said something and then wish you could take it back? I think all of us have. Controlling our tongues is one of the most important and most difficult communication challenges. If we all think before we speak then we will be in a much better place.

3. Decide that communication is a priority. If something is a priority then what do we usually give it? Time and Commitment.

4. Talk with people, not at them. Have you ever been talked *down* to? How did it make you feel? How did you feel at that moment about the person talking to you? Not too good, right? We need to talk *with* people. We need to make our communication conversational and user friendly. We need to ask ourselves, "How can I uplift this person as I express my thoughts and opinions?" This will help us communicate our messages in a more compassionate way. Even if we have to communicate some ugly message, compassion will see us through.

5. Have an open door policy. We must make time for people. If we lived in President Lincoln's day and wanted to speak with the president all we would have to do is walk in the White House and sit outside his door. When he came out, we would be able to speak with him. We need to do the same thing. If it worked for the president, it will work for us. If at that moment it is not appropriate, then make an appointment with the person.

6. Understand what Dale Carnegie & Associates, Inc. believe when they say, "Communication is built on trusting relationships." (*The Leader In You: How to Win Friends,*

Influence People, and Succeed in a Changing World by Stuart R. Levine, CEO, and Michael A. Crom, VP) If people don't trust us, then why would they listen to us?

7. Prepare, prepare, prepare. A number of years ago, I was trained by an organization called Speakers USA, Inc. They used to tell us that if we want a talk/presentation to look impromptu then make sure it is not. In other words, do your homework and prepare, prepare, prepare, practice, practice, practice.

8. Don't give a public presentation/talk unless you are passionate and knowledgeable about the topic. If we are not passionate about the topic then it will come across flat and boring. If we are not knowledgeable about the topic then our credibility will drop.

9. Make sure your body language, tone of voice, and message are congruent. Suppose I come up to you and say in a very gruff tone, "Sure, I would love to have the boss over for dinner!" Do you think I really want the boss to come over for dinner? You don't think so? Why? Because my tone and message aren't congruent. When we aren't congruent in every way, then we give mixed messages to our listeners.

10. Have patience. Communication, particularly public communication, is not easy. Be patient with yourself. You won't become an expert overnight. Keep practicing and keep improving.

11. Look for the benefit of our differences. We need to constantly remind ourselves that different doesn't necessarily mean wrong.

12. If agreement cannot be made then agree to disagree. It's a great way to keep the peace.

13. Keep your cool when someone improperly states something. They may not be trying to insult you. Have you ever thought you were being insulted but were not sure? Instead of reactively attacking back, just wait. They may have just said something in an awkward fashion. Don't jump to conclusions. Believe me, if they are actually trying to insult you and they think you don't get it, they will insult you again. And if they are insulting you then just simply tell them that you don't appreciate it and that you forgive them.

14. Always try to part on a positive upbeat ending. Nobody likes to leave with a sour attitude in his or her stomach. Always try to make peace before you end a conversation.

15. Loyalty many times comes from private conversations. Build trust by keeping confidences.

16. Use stories to illustrate your points. Jesus Christ always used stories when he taught the crowds. Abraham Lincoln believed in stories too. Lincoln said, "They say I tell a great many stories. I reckon I do; but I have learned from long experience that plain people, take them as they run, are more easily influenced through the medium of a broad and humorous illustration than in any other way." *REMEMBER: ALWAYS HAVE A POINT TO YOUR STORY.*

17. Learn to speak off the cuff (extemporaneously). Lincoln said, "Extemporaneously speaking should be practiced and cultivated…However able and faithful he may be in other respects, people are slow to bring him business if he cannot make a speech." One way to practice this is to grab your local paper and read a few headlines. Practice speaking on those topics for one to two minutes for each topic.

18. Join a Toastmasters club. Toastmasters International are speaking clubs designed to help people of all walks of life become more effective communicators and thus more successful. I was a member of Toastmasters for years and I really enjoyed and benefited from the experience. Check your local newspaper and/or library to find the club nearest you. If no luck there, then go to the World Wide Web at www.toastmasters.org. Plan to visit a local club as soon as you can. I don't think you will regret it.

19. Remember, we don't have to make a long speech in order to be effective. Just say what needs to be said and then stop talking. I remind you of Abraham Lincoln's Gettysburg Address.

20. Use Millard Bennett's 30-10 Power Formula. What is the 30-10 Power Formula? First you read for 30 minutes every day in whatever area you want to develop yourself in. This will build up your knowledge base. Of that 30 minutes, read out loud for 10 minutes. Reading out loud will improve your communication skills. It will improve your pronunciation, voice inflections, stamina, etc. Of that 10 minutes, read part of it in a whisper, maybe a minute or two. Reading in a whisper will eliminate all those umms, ahhs, and those other verbal fillers. This formula is one of the simplest formulas to practice but one of the most powerful. Try it for a month and see what you think.

21. Understand that an inspiring talk can change the face of an organization, nation, family, or an entire world. I remind you of Dr. Martin Luther King, Jr.'s "I have a dream" speech, JFK's challenge to put a man on the moon, and Reagan's "Mr. Gorbachov, tear down this wall."

I am convinced that if you really practice and work on these 21 steps you will become a POWER COMMUNICATOR and a greater success. Make it happen and have fun.

Pillar 2: Sales

Chapter Ten

Creating Value First

HOW WELL KNOWN is your funeral home? Do you have a lot of families who are loyal to you and refer your home to their friends? Or are you having trouble being noticed in a noisy world of marketing? Well, wherever you are on the spectrum, this chapter and the following chapters will share with you some simple ideas of expanding your list of customers. We are not going to talk about technical marketing strategies; just some simple, common sense marketing and sales you can put into practice at your funeral home today with great success.

Sales expert Jeffrey Gitomer says to always create value first. It is a good idea. Creating value first lessens the resistance from the prospective customer. So, how do we do this? Quite simply. Give something of value away. Really! It is that simple. Give value to a lot of people and a lot of people will be knocking on your door.

One way to do this is to give away a free sample, a free newsletter, a free consultation, etc. I know a chiropractor who does this very effectively by giving away a free body scan and consultation. He prints this free scan coupon on the back of his business card. Every time he gives out his business card he is adding value. Does it work? Absolutely!

I have a friend who calls this Serendipity Marketing. This is what he recommends and it works very well. Give away a free custom-designed blanket featuring photographs of your customer's loved one. Let me show you an example of what he is talking about:

My business friend said it works wonderfully in creating a "WOW" experience for the customer. Don't tell them you are doing this for them. Just surprise the family at the visitation or before the service.

Make sure they know you are giving it to them as a gift. If you would like to know more about this concept of Serendipity Marketing using custom blankets, give us a call at Bright

Corporation at 1-800-428-6424 and we will show you how to implement it at your funeral home.

As a Professional Speaker and Corporate Trainer, I sometimes give out a free 45-minute preview seminar. It lets a prospect test drive a seminar before they invest in a full seminar. I give them value by giving them ideas they can use immediately to be more effective. Does it work? Oh yeah! For example, I booked multiple days of seminars with one client using this technique.

Another idea to create value is to have a free newsletter. This can be a physical one you mail out or an email version called an ezine (make sure people have opted in to your email list or it is considered spam). Pack it full of helpful ideas that are of interest to your customers, their families, friends, and community. Give it away for free. Our electronic newsletter (ezine) *The Bright Newsletter* is packed monthly with powerful articles to help individuals, companies, and organizations be more effective and successful. We also give product discounts that only newsletter subscribers receive. You can get your free subscription at www.BrightCorporation.com.

Chapter Eleven

How to Create an Ocean of Referrals

YOUR LOYAL, happy families are your best source of new customers for your funeral home. Best-selling author Robert G. Allen said, "If you'll treat your customer like a star, you'll never have to spend another dime in advertising." He could not be more right. So, how do you treat your customers as stars?

Mark Victor Hansen, who is the co-creator of the *Chicken Soup for the Soul* series of books which has sold more than 100 million copies, tells the story of a dentist who discovered how to treat his patients as stars. Australian dentist Dr. Paddi Lund is the highest paid dentist in the world. But, not so long ago, it wasn't that way. Paddi was very, very depressed. He was working like a dog, he had 4,000 patients, and life wasn't much fun. In fact, he didn't even like a good deal of his patients. They got on his nerves.

Paddi took some time off and began reflecting on his life and his business. He decided that life was too short to be living it this way. He decided that he wasn't going to accept any patient that came in the door. He knew he needed to like and respect his patients and they needed to like and respect him.

When Paddi got back to work, he changed how business was done. First of all, he was going to treat his patients as friends. He began calling them by their first names and they began calling him Paddi. No more of this Dr. Lund stuff.

He hired a Director of Wonderful whose entire job was to greet patients as they entered the practice and to make sure they had a wonderful experience. Four times a day, fresh, hot cinnamon rolls would be rolled out for the patients who were waiting. If they liked them, they could even take them home. A $7,000 cappuccino machine sat ready and willing to refresh the customers with a warm, relaxing drink. Once a month, Paddi hosted a party where all his customers (friends) could get together and network with each other. Business as usual? Oh no, business changed dramatically.

Paddi now loves his customers and they love him too. He asks each of his patients to bring him three new patients a year who would love the same experience that they have at the dentist. Do you think his patients have a problem doing this for Paddi? No, they want to help. In fact, they love him so much, you couldn't tape their mouths shut. Paddi now has a waiting list to get into his practice. Oh, and by the way, Paddi only works 22 hours a week. You see, he owns the business. The business doesn't own him.

You can have the same type of business as Paddi Lund. How can you treat your customers as stars? It doesn't have to be cinnamon rolls, a cappuccino machine, or a Director of Wonderful. That works for Paddi. That may not work for you and your funeral home. What do you want? And more importantly, what does your customer want? Your best source of new customers comes from your happy, loyal families. Now, you have to be very gentle in asking for referrals in our industry. But it can be done.

In his *Success Mastery Academy* audio program, Brian Tracy teaches a four-step model for creating a "Golden Chain" of referrals. In a Golden Chain, one referral leads to another referral, and another, and another, and another.

THE FOUR-STEP REFERRAL PROCESS

1. Ask your customer if they know two or three people who they think would benefit from and be interested in your products and services. When you ask them for two or three they undoubtedly will choose two. That is why you ask for two or three. If you ask for one or two, they most likely will give you only one. Well, you might be saying, "Then why don't I ask for just three, or how about four?" The reason is that too many is intimidating. Two or three puts them at ease. Again, in our industry, you have to be gentle. Maybe ask them if they know two or three people who would benefit from your _____ (newsletter, custom designed blanket, coffee table book, etc.)

2. Ask your customer if they would happen to have their friend's telephone number. Most people will refer you to someone they like, and most likely they will have their telephone number handy.

3. Ask your customer which of these referrals they would suggest you contact first. (They will pick one.)

4. Ask your customer if they would call him or her and let them know you will be in touch with them. (Note: In our industry, I don't recommend doing this right away. Wait a while. Their grief is fresh. If you choose to ask this right away, I stress again: be very gentle.)

That is a four-step process and it might make you a little uncomfortable for a while, but it can double your sales and business in a very short time.

After you have contacted the person you were referred to, call back the person who gave you the referral. Thank them for the referral. Send them flowers, give them a gift, do something nice for them. Show them how much you appreciate them and the referral they gave you.

A "Golden Chain" of referrals. It takes a lot of discipline and a little courage, but it will change business as usual. Give it a try.

Chapter Twelve

The Law of the Farmer

**If you don't plant seeds today, you won't reap
a harvest... tomorrow!**

THE LAW of the Farmer is one of the great success truths of all time. You can find this truth in the ancient book of Matthew found in the Bible. The Great Teacher went down to the seashore and a huge crowd amassed around him. Everywhere He went, the crowds would gather. The Great Teacher looked over the crowd which was ready to hang onto His every word. He stepped into a small boat and was gently pushed a few feet from shore. In this way, the masses would not only be able to see Him more clearly, but would be able to hear Him more effectively as well.

The Great Teacher opened His mouth to speak. A hush came over the immense gathering of humanity. The Great Teacher said, "A farmer went out to plant some seed. As he scattered it across his field, some seeds fell on a footpath, and the birds came and ate them."

Let's stop right there and see what this has to say to us today. The seed fell on the path and birds came and ate the seed. Hmm? What does that mean? Well, I believe that some people get set in their ways. They like the old way of doing things. They like the old way of seeing things. And they like everything to stay the same. These people are not willing to change and grow. You position your product or service to this individual (you plant a seed). This person is so closed minded that they don't even see the opportunity, so the seed is stolen away, in this case by the birds.

Let me give you an example. For how many years have some medical doctors disagreed with the practice of chiropractic care? Too long to count. Many of them aren't even willing to consider the possibility that chiropractic care could help their patient. Their patient is not getting better but they would prefer to fail their patient than to open their eyes to refer them to a doctor of chiropractic. My family doctor is different. He had no problem with me seeing my chiropractor Dr. Paul Juszczyk. Why? Because his eyes are open.

Now, you might be thinking, "What if the person I am talking with is close-minded? What if my funeral home is selling pre-arrangements and they just don't understand why it is in their benefit to purchase now? What if they are the seed that falls on the path? What do I do?" My advice is do nothing. Move on to the next prospect. You see, their hardness of mind and heart is not your issue. It is theirs. You did your part. You planted a seed. In this case, it just didn't grow, and that is not your fault.

Let's get back to the story. The Great Teacher said, "Other seeds fell on shallow soil with underlying rock. The plants sprang up quickly, but they soon wilted beneath the hot sun and died because the roots had no nourishment in the shallow soil." What does this mean for us? Some prospects for your products and services get very excited about what they are hearing and seeing. The challenge for you is that they take no action. Because they do nothing, the motivation begins to fade away and in a very short time the seed begins to die. One of the ancient writings says, "But be doers of the word, and not hearers only, deceiving yourselves. For if anyone is a hearer of the word and not a doer, he is like a man observing his natural face in a mirror; for he observes himself, goes away, and immediately forgets what kind of man he was." Without action, many seeds will die. So, what should we do? Get the prospect to take action. Get them to make the appointment, fill out the form —it can be a number of things, but they must take action immediately or we will lose them.

The next part of the story reads, "Other seeds fell among thorns that shot up and choked out the tender blades." The thorns could be the other stresses in our lives that preoccupy our minds. When a prospect has a thorn there is not much you can do. The timing may be wrong. You did everything you could possibly do. You planted your seed. Now, it is a waiting game. Contact the prospect on a regular basis to stay in touch. But don't just call them up and say, "Hi. Just wanted to give you a call to touch base." Yuk! You must give them value. That is why I like newsletters and ezines. They are a great way to stay in touch and at the same time add value for them. Pack your newsletters with helpful articles that are going to improve their lives and reduce the stress (the thorns).

The Great Teacher finishes His story with, "But some seeds fell on fertile soil and produced a crop that was thirty, sixty, and even a hundred times as much as had been planted. Anyone who is willing to hear should listen and understand." Why do some seeds produce more than others? I haven't a clue. But the truth is that some do and we don't have to be concerned with the "why." All we have to do is plant the seeds, water and fertilize them, and be ready to bring in the harvest.

Another time, the Great Teacher said, "Keep on asking, and you will be given what you ask for. Keep on looking and you will find. Keep on knocking, and the door will be opened. For everyone who asks, receives. Everyone who seeks, finds. And the door is opened to everyone who knocks." I think this teaches us not to give up. To be persistent. If you are digging for gold, you will have to uncover a lot of dirt to find a nugget, but if you keep asking, seeking, and knocking, you will find the nugget. And the nugget is always worth it. It was Calvin Coolidge who said, "Nothing in the world can take the place of persistence. Talent will not; nothing is more common than the unsuccessful man with talent. Genius will not; unrewarded genius is almost a proverb. Education will not; the world is full of educated derelicts. Persistence and determination alone are omnipotent." Stay the course and you will be successful. The Law of the Farmer works and it will work for you, too.

Chapter Thirteen

The Law of Averages

If you put your message in front of one person, you will reap a small harvest. If you put your message in front of 10,000 people, you will reap a larger harvest.

UNDERSTANDING and using the Law of Averages leads to more sales and customers for your funeral home. How? When you take an action enough times, a ratio of statistics will begin to introduce itself. Let me explain.

I grew up in Indiana where basketball is king. In fact, my hometown of Anderson has the second-largest high school basketball gym in the nation. The "Wigwam" holds just under 9,000 people. The largest high school gym is just 30 minutes down the road in New Castle, Indiana where their field house seats around 9,300 people. We take our basketball seriously. We also use the Law of Averages. One place we use the law of averages is at the free throw line. A coach always wants their player with the best free throw percentage on the line at the end of the game. Games are won and lost at the free throw line.

Games are won and lost in the business world, too. Not at the free throw line, but in how we use the Law of Averages. Let's say that you talk to one hundred people about prearranging their funeral needs. Two out of those one hundred become new customers of yours. Now you have a ratio. Two out of every one hundred people that you talk with will become a customer. That is exciting! Why? Because the Law of Averages tends to repeat itself. It is consistent. There is a great chance that if you talk with another hundred people, you will gain two more new customers.

I know what you are thinking, "Mark, how can you be so excited? It is only two percent." Yes, it is only two percent, but it is a place to start. In time, it might be four percent, and then eight percent, and so on. How do you change the Law of Averages? By getting better. By growing. By learning Influence, Leadership, and Sales skills. Also, we have to remember that those original two percent are going to talk about us. So, if we develop them into loyal customers then that word of mouth is going to bring in even more new customers. Remember the Serendipity Marketing we talked about in an earlier chapter?

There is also a lot of other ways to market. What if you reached your prospects by sending out direct mail pieces and postcards, voice broadcasts, billboards, etc.? How we use the Law of Averages can be endless. It also helps us know how to use our marketing and sales dollars best. Let's say that we send out two different postcards to one thousand people each time. By using the Law of Averages, we can see which postcard works best. A change in the wording or a change of look can make a big difference in the response rate. The Law of Averages can make or break your business. Begin to use it for your advantage and you will be amazed how much more successful your funeral home will become.

Chapter Fourteen

Sales Presentations and Closing the Sale

THE SALES PRESENTATION is one of the most important communication skills that we can learn. Whether we are selling a product, service, ourselves, our ideas, or even selling someone on where to go out to eat, how we influence with our communication determines to a great degree the results we will achieve.

In this chapter, I am going to share with you some of the ideas I have learned on sales communication throughout the years. Nothing here is original with me. I just want to pass on to you what I have learned from the experts. The sales experts I refer to include Brian Tracy, Zig Ziglar, Tom Hopkins, John Hammond, and others. So, let's lean on them and improve our communication and close more sales.

FINDING OUT WHO THE DECISION MAKER IS

When it comes to presenting your ideas in a sales situation, the first thing we have to do is make sure we are talking with the right person. We could talk all day and do a marvelous job of convincing the other person of our ideas, but if that person isn't the decision maker then it is all for nothing. We have to make sure we are selling to the right person, the person who can make the decision. So, how do we find the right person? Let's say you are calling an organization but you aren't sure who you need to talk with. For example, you could say this:

Good morning/afternoon! This is <u>Your Name</u>. I am not sure who I need to speak with so maybe you can point me in the right direction. I need to talk with whoever is in charge of _____. Do you know who that is?

Or (a more direct approach):

Good morning/afternoon. This is <u>Your Name.</u> Who is the person in your organization in charge of _____?

Wait for them to answer. Then ask politely if you can speak to that person.

Another important thing to clarify is if they can make the decision independently or someone else is also involved in the process. Once you find the decision maker(s), now is the time to present your ideas.

When the decision maker answers the phone or door, it is always polite to ask if this is a good time. If it is not, attempt to set an appointment with them. If now is a good time, it is time to present your ideas.

THE SALES PRESENTATION

Your first objective in the sales presentation is to ask them a question they have to answer with a "yes." It needs to be a question that brings home your key benefit. For example, in one of my businesses of presenting Sales Success Training Seminars, I might say something like:

I was wondering if you would be interested in a proven system that can increase your sales by 20 to 40 percent over the next twelve months.

Or

I was wondering if you would be interested if I could show you a way to increase your sales by 20 to 40 percent over the next twelve months.

If I am talking with the Sales Manager or the Vice President of Sales then they have to answer "yes" to those questions. In their mind, the prospect is thinking, "Of course I want that. How can I get it?" They only respond that way if they are the decision maker for that area. I could use the same above questions with the Vice President of Human Resources for a company and the questions would wither on the vine. Why? Because selling is not in their wheelhouse and they don't care as much about sales success.

The next thing you want to do is ask the prospect questions. Here is a key phrase to memorize: **Questions Open Doors**. Too many sales professionals talk too much. It is much more important for the prospect to do most of the talking. Here are some sample questions you might want to ask your prospect:

What are you doing now in the area of _____?

Would it be easier on your children if you took care of your prearrangement needs now instead of them having to work out the details later?

How is that working for you?

If you could have anything you wanted, what results would you like to achieve in the next 12 months?

Mr./Ms. Prospect, if ever you were to choose to use our program or any other company's program, what would lead you to make that decision? (This question identifies their "Hot Button" or their "Key Benefit." Once you find what this is, sell this benefit of your program or idea.)

HOW TO CLOSE THE SALE

Closing the sale is all about overcoming objections. Zig Ziglar said, "I can state with considerable confidence that in most cases involving significant purchases, if you do not encounter objections from the prospect when you make your presentation, you do not have a prospect." He is right. If they don't object somewhere, they probably aren't the decision maker or are not interested in your offer at all. So, how do we turn their objections into a "yes" for your offer? In this section, we are going to lean heavily on the wisdom of experts Zig Ziglar and John Hammond. Adapt the following closes to your offer and you will be on your way to great selling success.

"Assume that they will buy" Close

Mr./Ms. Prospect, when we prearrange your funeral needs, we will walk with you every step of the way making sure that we take care of all your wishes and desires which will in turn give your family a great deal of peace when the time comes. And that's what you really want, isn't it?

If they say "yes" to this question, go ahead and finish the deal (pull out the contract, set the appointment/date, etc.)

"Your price is too high/costs too much" Close

If the prospect says, "It costs too much," then you say,

I agree with you, Mr. Prospect, that good _____ isn't cheap and cheap _____ isn't good. My funeral home had a choice. We decided we would rather explain price one time than apologize for poor quality _____ forever. I am sure you are glad we made that decision, aren't you?

Wait for their response. If it is favorable, then close the sale. If they are still hesitant, then continue with this next statement and question.

It is true that we all should invest in the best at the beginning and get the results that work rather than pay for the cheap now and forever because the results weren't there. Wouldn't you agree?

Wait for their response. If it is favorable, then proceed to close the sale. You can also remind them—if you are selling prearrangements—that they are investing at today's dollars which will save them on inflation prices when the time comes.

"Three Question" Close

Mr./Ms. Prospect, can you see how this _____ will help your team be more successful at Key Benefit?

Are you interested in them being more successful at <u>Key Benefit</u>?

When do you think is a good time for them to begin being more successful at <u>Key Benefit</u>?

Wait for the prospect's response after each question. These questions can be tailored to fit almost any selling situation.

"Talking Pad" Close

Zig Ziglar talks about using a "talking pad." A Talking Pad is a tablet or sheet of paper on which you can write the prospect's objections. If the prospect hits you with more than one question (objection), then you pull out a pad of paper and write down their questions in an abbreviated form. Then say,

If I understand you correctly Mr./Ms. Prospect, your questions (don't say objections) are _____, _____, and _____. Is that correct?

Wait for their agreement. If they don't agree, then find out what the real questions are. If they do agree, then say,

In other words, Mr./Ms. Prospect, if you can convince yourself that _____, _____, and _____ (wording them in the positive, for example: "That our price is fair, we can service your account, and that our _____ will give you the results you want") *then you would be comfortable with us _____. Is that what you are saying?*

You then proceed to answer their questions. After you have answered each question—pause— and ask the prospect if that answers their question. If their response is favorable then ask their permission to cross out that question from your talking pad. Continue the same procedure with their other questions. When all questions have been crossed off your talking pad, what else is there to do except fill out the contract or provide them with what you are selling.

"Your product is just like…" Close

Every once in a while, the prospect will compare your product, service, or idea with one at another funeral home. The prospect will say something like, "Your _____ is just like …" When the prospect says this, don't argue with them or deny it. Find a point of agreement. Say,

Yes, I agree with you Mr./Ms. Prospect, there are some similarities between our _____ , which is what you are saying, isn't it? (Wait for their agreement.) Then continue (this is a tailored response that works for me because it is about me), *Mr./Ms. Prospect, let me give you an example. I am a trumpet player. I own a Bach Stradivarius Trumpet. When comparing my Bach Stradivarius trumpet with a beginning student horn the visible differences are minute; however, when you compare the sound and quality of the instruments, the differences are profound. Mr./Ms. Prospect, we are the Bach Stradivarius of our industry. You do want the best _____ at the best price, don't you?* (This is an example that fits my life. Tailor your response to fit your life.)

Wait for their answer. If it is positive, then proceed to close the sale. If it is not positive, find out what the real concern is.

Let me end this chapter with some great closing ideas from sales legend John Hammond. He has been very helpful and influential to me and my career, and I know his ideas will be for yours as well.

LET'S BE

REVERSE ANSWER TECHNIQUE   Use this any time the prospect uses the word "too" (for example, "It's too much money"). You say, *Yes, Mr./Ms. Prospect, it does require an investment. That is why it's a good idea to start now.*

EXPLAIN IT   Just explain the objection away.

ADMIT IT   We cannot be everything for everyone. Our product/service doesn't have to solve every need to still be sold to the prospect. Answer the objection this way*: Yes, Mr./Ms. Prospect, you are correct. We do not have/do _____. We think our _____ other features/benefits outweigh that one area. Don't you agree?*

DENIAL   We have to stand up for something. Not everyone will buy and not everyone is the ideal prospect for you.

Y WHY?   Some prospects will repay your kindness by not telling you the truth. They do this because they don't want to hurt you by rejecting your product/service or idea. When this happens ask yourself, "Was the reason this prospect gave me clearly stated?" For example, the prospect might say, "I want to think it over." Then do three things: 1. Smile 2. Say, *"Obviously Mr./Ms. Prospect, you have a good reason for saying that (or feeling this way). Do you mind if I ask what it is?"* 3. Be quiet. Let the prospect answer.

TO ANSWER OBJECTIONS!

Pillar 3: Customer Service

Chapter Fifteen

Satisfied Customers are Absolutely Worthless

THE LATE CHAPLAIN of the United States Senate, Peter Marshall, used to tell a story titled *The Keeper of the Springs*. The story is about a man who lived in a forest in the eastern Alps overlooking an Austrian village. This old man had been hired years ago by a wise town council to make sure the river flowing through the quaint village continued to bring fresh, clean water from the mountain springs which were its source.

The old man faithfully year after year removed leaves, twigs, and everything that could contaminate or clog the mountain springs. As a result, the village river was an attraction for vacationers and swans alike. The village was peaceful, happy, and blessed.

One night, years later, another town council began talking about the almost-mythical keeper of the springs. They wondered, "Why are we paying this man? Does anyone ever see him? This money could be used for better purposes." As a result, you can imagine what they did. They decided to terminate the services of the old man.

For a while, everything stayed the same. The river was beautiful and the village blossomed. But then came autumn, and the trees began to lose their grip on their leaves. Twigs and branches broke off the trees and fell into the pools around the springs.

One day, someone noticed something different about their wonderful river. It was changing to a different color. Soon a haze came over parts of the river and a sickening smell began to hover around it. The vacationers left the lovely village. The swans decided to look for a new home.

The town council called an emergency meeting. They realized what a terrible mistake they had made by firing the old man of the forest. They immediately hired him back. The old man got to work and performed the miracle again. Within a few weeks, clean, life-giving water was flowing freely and surely from the springs to the village river. Soon all was normal, healthy, and blessed.

Now, you might be thinking, "This is kind of an odd way to start this section of the book. What does that story have to do with me and my funeral home?" My answer to that question is *everything*. You see, you, your team, and your funeral home are the village river. Your customers are the mountain springs. The truth of the matter is that if you don't take care of your mountain springs, it will put a strangle hold on your village river. It will sicken, smell, and if something is not done to reverse the process it will eventually die.

Right here at the very beginning of this section, I want you to think about your mountain springs. Are those families loyal to you or do they see your funeral home as a dime-a-dozen?

But before you panic, don't worry. That is why I have written this section of the book. And that is why Customer Service is one of *The 3 Pillars of Success*. We are first going to put the lid on your village spring. In other words, I am going to help you get rid of *satisfied* customers and turn them into *loyal* customers.

Satisfied customers are worthless. They stay just until the next big thing comes to town. Let's say that your customer lives ten miles from your funeral home and one of your competitors moves in just one mile away from your customer's home. Guess what happens? If they are merely satisfied, they are not your customer anymore. If that family is loyal, they are not going to jump ship. They will continue to use you for their funeral needs.

I am a patient of Juszczyk Chiropractic in Lebanon, Ohio. Do you know how far I drive to have my adjustments? I drive about 25 minutes one way. Why? First of all, Dr. Paul is good. Very good. I have some major back injuries, much of it caused by years of competition tennis. Dr. Paul has taken me from tremendous pain to a lot of relief. We are not out of the woods yet, but I can see the sunshine. But that alone doesn't keep me with Juszczyk. There are a lot of great doctors of chiropractic. I am loyal because Dr. Paul is not only a great doctor; he has also become a friend. He has connected with me. He cares about me and my family. That is why I am loyal. And now, he has made it even more convenient. He has opened a second office just minutes from my house.

We just finished the Second Pillar of Success which was Sales. But I want to make crystal clear that the Three Pillars work *together* to support your funeral home's success. The truth of the matter is that loyal customers create more customers. Loyal customers become your best marketing.

Loyal customer Bob is minding his own business eating his lunch in the company cafeteria, when coworker Sally starts talking about how her teenage daughter Cathy needs to have braces on her teeth. Sally tells Bob that her dentist said Cathy needs braces and soon. Sally is frustrated because she doesn't know what orthodontist to take Cathy to. She tells Bob that her dentist recommends five good ones in the area. But she doesn't want to play Russian roulette with the five. Who should she choose?

Bob says to Sally, "Who are the five orthodontists? Maybe I can help you choose. My son David had to get braces two years ago. We went to Dr. Kevin Baxter and he was great."

"Dr. Baxter?" exclaims Sally. "His name is one of the five orthodontists my dentist recommends."

"I would have no challenge recommending him. David loved him."

"Dr. Baxter it is. Thanks Bob. I owe you one."

"Don't mention it. Glad to help."

Loyal customers create new customers. New customers become loyal customers and create more new customers. And the cycle goes on and on and on. So, let's get started. Let's back up to the beginning…and let's create some loyal customers.

Chapter Sixteen

What is Customer Service?

THE FIRST THING we have to do is to define our goal. What is customer service? Once we can define it then we can pin point like a laser beam the direction and focus of your funeral home.

After teaching hundreds of seminars, I have discovered that one of the best ways to discover excellent customer service is by putting ourselves in our customers' shoes. If you were in their situation what would you want?

We are all customers. We all shop. We all go out to eat. And we are all patients. So, what do you want?

Let's make two lists. On the first list, I want you to list all the things that tick you off as a customer. Things that irritate you. Things that drive you away from one business into the arms of another.

The Things that Irritate Me as a Customer

What did you write down in this category? You may have put down things such as rude attendants, having to wait a long time, and poor quality products and services. Let me mention one of my pet peeves: the Automated Phone System. You know what I am talking about. Those systems that say something like this, "If you want to talk to so and so then press 1, if you want to talk to so and so then press 2…" Then, once you finally push a button, what does it do to you? It sends you to another menu.

Finally, you reach a live person, but what is your attitude now? You're ticked, right? Many times, the systems we have in place to make our lives easier actually create ticked-off customers and thus create havoc and stress in our own lives.

I've mentioned my family owns the Bright Corporation in Anderson, Indiana. Besides being an author and seminar leader, I am also a Vice President at the company. If you aren't familiar with us, we sell papered products (register books, memorial folders, acknowledgement cards, etc.) to the funeral industry. I bring this up because if you were to call the Bright Corporation during business hours, you would get a live person. Why? Because we are adamant about this. When my grandfather bought this business over seventy years ago the business was housed in a garage. That is all the larger it was. My family built it up from the ground floor. Today, the company ships products all across the United States and even a little beyond its borders. It has been built up by the personal relationship with each customer.

Now, there are challenges of having a philosophy of answering the phone with a live person. The main challenge is that you have to have someone available to answer the phone during all business hours. Is it worth it? You can count on it. Many times, the things that irritate us as customers will irritate our own customers as well. We have to make sure we aren't putting up barriers between us and a relationship with our customers.

For our second list, let's write down the things we customers love.

The Things I love as a Customer

You can have my pants

Let me share with you something I loved as a customer. A number of years ago, I had a very strange experience on a speaking engagement in Indianapolis. Since I was still living in Anderson, Indiana at the time, about 40 miles northeast of Indy, I decided I would grab one of my suits and drive down the night before and stay in the Hyatt Regency where the seminar was going to be held the next day.

I was relaxing in my hotel room and something hit me—you better check your suit. I got up and walked to the closet in my hotel room. At first glance, the suit looked fine. After more detailed scrutiny, I realized I didn't have any pants. What happened to my pants? I knew I had pants when I left home. Where could they be? I then realized what had happened. I had carried my suit in a hanging bag from the cleaners. The type that has no bottom to it. My pants had fallen off the hanger somewhere between my home and the hotel room.

What was I going to do without any pants? Well, I decided I had better look in the hotel. I went down to the parking garage and retraced my steps—no pants! I then went to the front desk and asked if anyone had found any pants. You can imagine the looks I got.

This particular Hyatt Regency also had stores in it. I looked around and unfortunately all of them were closed at this time of night. I asked the front desk what time the shops opened in the morning. Big problem! Too late the next day to be of help to me. Then something amazing happened. A young man behind the front desk heard what was going on. He said, "I have some pants in the back. You can wear my pants." TALK ABOUT SERVICE! I wore this guy's pants all the next day. They were a little big, but at least I had pants.

When is the last time you gave your pants to your customer? Not lately, huh! Well, too bad. You see, look back at the story you just read. Do you see something in it? What was the name of the hotel I was staying at? It is there, isn't it? I have no problem (in fact, I love doing it) boosting up the business of Hyatt Hotels. The truth of the matter is that you don't have a problem either. Word of mouth advertising is the best kind of advertising and it starts with great service.

So, how do we encompass everything we love as customers and how do we keep from doing to our customers everything we hate as customers? I have a two-pronged definition of customer service. A definition that encompasses everything we have talked about thus far and everything we will talk about.

Great Customer Service Is:

1. Finding a need and filling it

2. Doing for the customer what you know they want done for them.

Let's break this down a bit. First, **finding a need and filling it**. What does this really mean? Have you ever heard the saying that the customer is always right? Of course you have. Your customers keep preaching that to you. But I'll let you in on a little secret. It's not true. That quote has been taken out of context for years. In fact, it is only half the original quote. The challenge is that you have probably only heard it that way, and even more challenging is that your customers have only heard it that way, too.

The entire quote was from Marshall Field and he actually said, "Right or wrong, the customer is always right." This means something totally different. You see, your customer may not always be right, but they are still the customer.

Sam Walton of Walmart perfected this. Sam understood that his customers weren't always right, but he more importantly understood that they were the King, the Queen,…the Boss. Sam understood that he worked for the customer.

Every once in a while, a customer would walk into the door of a Walmart and say, "I need this...." When in all actuality, that wasn't what they needed at all. They needed something totally different. You see, finding a need and filling it doesn't mean you give the customer everything they *say* they need. That may not be right for them. The key word in Customer Service is *service*. What if Sam gave the customer what they said they needed and then six weeks down the road, they discovered it didn't work? Who are they upset with? Right, good ole Sam and Walmart.

What I mean by finding a need and filling it is finding and filling the customer's *true* need. What are the results they are looking for? When it is all said and done, where do they want to be? That is their true need and that is the need we need to fill. Now, I will admit, this makes your initial job tougher. You have to connect with the customer. Your bedside manner has to be awesome. You need to communicate with that customer and help them understand why your approach will work in giving them the results they are looking for.

Two, **do for that customer what you know they want done for them.** Many of us were taught the Golden Rule as children. That is exactly what this is. Well, how do we find out what they really want? The first thing we can do is what we have already done in this book. What do you want as a customer? What do you like and what irritates you? That is the first clue for what they want. The second clue can be attained by simply asking them. Ask the customer. "What can I do for you today, Mr./Ms. Customer?"

The first thing we have to do to achieve that worthy goal is to connect with the customer. If we can't connect with them then it is already over. In the next chapter, we are going to discuss just how to build rapport with the customer.

Chapter Seventeen

Why We Must Connect With the Customer

A NUMBER of years ago, research was done to discover why customers will stop doing business with an organization. The statistics were quite interesting. This is what was discovered.

Why Customers Leave...or Want To!	
1%	die
3%	move away
4%	are fickle and float
5%	listen to their friend's advice
9%	can buy product/service cheaper somewhere else
10%	are complainers and whiners
68%	feel we do not care about their needs

Rapport – The Answer to Connection

The answer to this dilemma is rapport. We have to connect with the customer if we want a chance of making them loyal. Have you ever wished you knew how to get along better with people? Have you ever wanted to connect with a perfect stranger? But how can we connect better? How do we build rapport with people?

In the 1930s, Dale Carnegie wrote a terrific book titled *How to Win Friends and Influence People.* His book has a section filled with six steps to get people to like us. That is what rapport really is. When we like someone and they like us then we have rapport and trust with each other. In this chapter, let us use Dale Carnegie's six steps as our guide to rapport. It's a guideline to connection with not only our customers but everyone in our lives from the perfect stranger to our best friend.

STEP #1: Be sincerely interested in other people.

Have you ever been talking to someone and knew that in their mind they were two thousand miles away? How did that make you feel? Like you were being taken for granted? Well, we want to make sure we don't make other people feel that way. We need to be sincerely interested in other people. This is not easy. Research shows that many people are focused primarily on their own needs, desires, and wants. I know I have to fight that temptation. As champions, we must go against this grain. We must put our needs (at least temporarily) aside and become sincerely interested in other people. If we can do this then we will start building better rapport with other people.

STEP #2: Simply smile.

Are you a dog lover? If you are, you will probably understand this. When you get home at night what does your dog do? He probably greets you at the door with his tail wagging and his tongue sticking out. In its mind, the dog is thinking, "Where have you been? I am so glad you are home. Do you want to play some ball? I do! Do you? Oh, I love you, I love you, I love you. Please never leave me again!" To build rapport, we need to be more like a puppy dog. Now, don't slobber on people, but we do need to greet people properly. We need to smile people into our lives.

A smile softens, it opens the door to the heart. When that door is open, connection has been made. We need to commit our lives to giving away as many smiles each day as possible. Give it a try. I believe you will discover that you have more connection with people and even feel better yourself. Not only will you feel good because you have brightened someone's day but it will also brighten your day physically. The muscles that form a smile actually release a chemical in your brain that makes you feel good. Isn't that great!

You might be thinking, "That's great, Mark, but I spend most of my day on the telephone. Does a smile help me build rapport?" The answer is a resounding "YES!" There are telemarketing companies that put a mirror on the desk of the people who are on the phone all day. Why do they do that? Because employees looking at their own sour face all day long will probably start to smile. When they smile, it brightens their tone and they build rapport with the customer on the other end of the phone line. A smile or a frown can be heard by the customer no matter how many miles of phone line are between them and you.

STEP #3: Honor a person's name

Dale Carnegie said that the sweetest sound in any language is the sound of our own name. Get into the habit of using a person's name in conversation with them. Don't use it every other sentence because that will annoy them, but two or three times in a conversation will connect with them. Also, don't forget to use their name in the middle of letters, memos, or emails. For example, your note might look as follows.

Dear Bob,
Fantastic job on the xyz project. So and so was sold by your presentation. (At this point, the note continues)...

Bob, ...(Here you are using Bob's name again before making your statement.)

STEP #4: Be a listener.

Dale Carnegie shared the story of how a department store in Chicago, Illinois almost lost a valued customer. Mrs. Douglas spent thousands of dollars every year in this one particular department store. One day she walked into the store and bought a coat that was on sale. When she got home, she realized the coat had a rip in the lining. That obviously upset her. She went back to the store and showed the ripped lining to a sales clerk. The clerk pointed to a sign and gruffly said, "All sales are final! If you don't like it then you can sew it up yourself."

"But it is damaged," said Mrs. Douglas.

"Doesn't matter! Sold means sold!"

Mrs. Douglas was about to leave the store and probably not return when she ran across the department store manager. The manager knew her very well because of her loyal years of shopping there. The manager did something that honored her. He just listened. He let her share everything that was on her chest. He let her share the anger that was bubbling up inside her and her disappointment in the product. Once Mrs. Douglas had said everything she wanted to say, the manager spoke. He said, "Mrs. Douglas, it is true that on sale items the sales are final so we can clear our merchandise at the end of a season. But that policy has nothing to do with damaged merchandise. By all means we will replace the item for you, fix it, or give you your money back. Whichever you prefer."

Couldn't the store manager have said this at the very beginning of their conversation? Sure, but that would have solved only part of the problem. You see, Mrs. Douglas needed to feel understood, and the best way to help someone feel understood is too simply listen to him or her. Many times people just need to be heard.

STEP #5: Talk in terms of their interests.

In Step One we learned we need to be genuinely interested in other people. In this step we will learn to talk in terms of their interest. For example, do you have a coworker who just got back from vacation? If so, ask them about it. Do you have a friend who loves to go sailing? If so, ask them if they have been able to get out on the boat lately with the kids. You see, these are things they love to do. These are things they also love to talk about. When we are willing to talk in terms of another person's interest, it fuels their enthusiasm for life. That enthusiasm will bubble over into the conversation we want to have with them.

STEP #6: Make them feel important and do it sincerely.

Have you ever been invited to a party and as soon as you walked in the door, the host said, "Wow! You look great. You haven't changed a bit. You look awesome." For about a minute, you feel very special—until you hear them saying the same thing to the next person who walks in the door. That's called false flattery, and that will destroy your rapport.

So, how do we make someone feel important and do it sincerely? Let me give you an example. When I was in college, I was in Air Force ROTC (Reserve Officers Training Corps). We had to give a speech in our military history course. For many people, public speaking is a fear worse than death. But believe me, it's even more intimidating to have to give a speech in front of a full-fledged colonel who is your commanding officer. I would have been thrilled if Colonel Biltz had pulled me aside when I was done and said, "You did a great job, Cadet Bowser." But he didn't do that. He actually did something even more honoring for me. He set me up as an example for the rest of the cadets in the class. Colonel Biltz said something like this, "This is what Cadet Bowser did well and what we can learn from it." He used me as an example on how to be prepared and give a fine presentation. That definitely made me feel important.

What Colonel Biltz did was give me a sincere compliment. Colonel Biltz (and most colonels, for that matter) aren't the kind of people who are going to give you false flattery. They will give you a compliment when you deserve it and encouragement when you need it. We can follow Colonel Biltz's example and make people feel important. Who can you give a lift to today? Catch them doing something right and praise them for it.

Well, there you have it, my friend. Six steps to transform your relationships. If we really want to connect with people all we have to do is:

> ## How to Connect with People
> 1. Be sincerely interested in other people
> 2. Simply smile
> 3. Honor a person's name
> 4. Be a listener
> 5. Talk in terms of their interests
> 6. Make them feel important and do it sincerely

Now, it is up to you. Go out there and make it happen!

Chapter Eighteen

Responsibility: The Buck Stops···Where?

THERE IS a customer service philosophy known as **under promise; over deliver.** It is one of the secrets of success. If this philosophy is so important, then what does it mean and how do we live it? Let's break it down and take a look at it.

First of all, I believe it means we have to give ourselves a little grace period. Let's say it normally takes you two days to do something for a customer. What I recommend is telling them that you will have it done for them no later than three days. Why three days? Because there is a little guy named Murphy. Now, from time to time Murphy comes to visit us. He brings with him his own little law known as Murphy's Law which basically says if something can go wrong, it will. If you said you would have it done for them in two days and Murphy comes and messes everything up and you're late, then your customer is upset and your credibility is weakened. On the other hand, if you say you will have it done no later than three days and Murphy shows up and delays the progress, you still have a chance of getting it done on time because you have given yourself a little grace period. Don't expect everything to go perfect all the time.

By saying no later than three days, you give yourself options anywhere between day one and day three. What if you tell them you will have it done for them no later than three days and Murphy doesn't show up and you get it done for your customer in two days? Your customer is thrilled. You are terrific. I know there are going to be times when you can't give yourself a grace period, but when you can, under promise; over deliver.

The next thing this philosophy says to me is that we have to take responsibility. United States President Truman had a sign on his desk. Do you remember what it said? **"The Buck Stops Here!"** President Truman made that popular, but do you know the historical heritage of that statement? It goes farther back in history than Truman. Where it comes from is from the old days when they were playing cards. They would put a buck knife in front of the next dealer. The buck stops here. The responsibility stops here. Over the years, they quit using the buck knife. They would use a coin instead, like a silver dollar. They still referred to it as a buck. That is why you might say that you have ten bucks in your pocket.

Years later, President Truman put that sign on his desk saying that he was taking responsibility for everything in his administration. If something went wrong, then he would fix it. If he couldn't fix it then he would take the heat. The buck stopped with him. He was responsible. Where does the buck stop in our lives? Are we always looking for a scapegoat? Do we always have an excuse? Is it always someone else's fault? The champion has the courage to take responsibility and action to back it up. The buck stops with us!

The third element I believe we can take from this philosophy is that we must **"go the extra mile."** You have probably heard that statement all your life, but do you know the historical perspective on this one? Let me give you a hint. It is older than the last one. Doesn't help? Well, why don't I go ahead and tell you. This saying is around 2,000 years old. It is a biblical phrase.

It comes from the teachings of Jesus Christ. It has to do with Roman law.

In Jesus' day, Roman law said that if a Roman soldier came up to you and said, "Carry my armor!", then by law you were required to carry his armor for one mile. If you didn't comply he could probably kill you. So, as you can imagine, most people carried the armor but they weren't too pleased about it. They weren't too fond of the Roman soldiers. Rome was a conqueror. These soldiers were a representation of their bondage. They despised the soldiers. So, they weren't too pleasant as they carried the armor.

Well, Jesus turned things upside down. He told the people of Israel to carry the armor not only one mile but two miles. Give them more than they expect. Shock them with kindness. Give that extra effort. Be nice to the Roman soldiers. Talk with them. Connect with them. The result of this was fantastic. History records that when Christianity was spread to the Roman Empire, it was spread through the Roman soldiers. The Christians had gone the extra mile in the Roman soldiers' lives and impacted them forever. The Roman soldiers in turn went back home and influenced more lives.

When we give that little extra effort, spend that extra moment with a customer, or do something that needs to be done even though it is not our job to do it, then wonderful things happen. It changes not only the lives we touch, it changes ours as well.

"WE'LL GET IT PAINTED FOR YOU!"

I had a friend who really taught me what it means to "go the extra mile." His name was C.A. Bridges. Unfortunately, he passed away way too soon. At the time of this story, C.A. was the service manager at Tom Wood Lexus in Indianapolis,

Indiana. A number of years ago, I was having trouble with my car. The clear coat was peeling off the hood of my Chevrolet Beretta. The car looked like it had sunburn. So I went to my local dealer and I showed them the paint problem. The body guy said, "That kind of paint problem doesn't fall under our warranty." In other words, I was out of luck. I would have to pay for it myself.

Well, I was sharing this challenge with C.A. and he let me vent, and then he said, "I think we can help you out at Lexus. Bring the car in to me and we will get it painted, and you won't have to pay for it." C.A. explained that the body work guy at Tom Wood Lexus also does overflow body work at Dan Young Chevrolet, also in Indianapolis.

So, I drove my very badly painted Chevy Beretta onto this luxury car lot. I'll have to admit, it kind of stood out. I don't think they left it outside very long, for obvious reasons. What I think they did behind the scenes was take the car to Dan Young Chevrolet to be worked on. When there was a delay in finishing the car, C.A. even arranged for me to get a rental car free of charge. When the car was done, I drove off in a very beautifully painted Chevrolet Beretta.

What did I get out of this experience? I got help. I got help in an area I couldn't help myself in. What did C.A. get out of this? Well, I am sure he got that warm feeling most of us get when we help someone in an area we know they couldn't help themselves in. How about Tom Wood Lexus? I wasn't one of their customers. What did they get out of this? For one thing, they get a lot of publicity. I have shared this story with seminar audiences all over the country. I also just shared it with you in this book. But they didn't do it for that reason. You see, this was years ago and my speaking schedule was not near as full as it is today. There was very little PR to give. Also, I don't think Tom

Wood himself ever knew this took place. He has empowered his team to do the right thing —to go the extra mile.

Under promise; over deliver! What a concept. If every individual and every organization would adopt this philosophy then our success would be guaranteed. So, where does the buck stop? It stops with us! Success is our choice.

Chapter Nineteen

How to Deal with Difficult People

HAVE YOU ever had a difficult customer? One of those who you wish would become someone else's customer? Well, unfortunately, we all have had customers like that. What we all need to do is to begin looking at it as an opportunity instead of a negative. In this chapter, we are going to look at the "whys" of looking at them as an opportunity and the "dos" of handling them more effectively and positively.

First, let's look at the "whys." A number of years ago the White House Council on Consumer Affairs performed a research project that to this day has some chilling news for us. The White House council discovered (depending on industry, part of the country in which you live, etc.) that it can cost five or six times more to get a new customer than to keep a current customer. You may have dealt with the same family for generations. You are their funeral home of choice for all their family members. The message is clear. Just for pure economic reasons, we need to do everything we can to keep the customers we have even if they can be a pain in the rear sides of our anatomy.

The White House Council also discovered that 96 percent of unhappy customers won't tell us when they're unhappy. Uh-oh! Big problem! Now, here is an even bigger problem. The Council found out that 91 percent of the 96 percent unhappy customers will go somewhere else to be served if we don't resolve their challenges to their satisfaction.

Now, I know what you are thinking: "Mark, if they don't tell me that they are upset and dissatisfied, how in the world am I supposed to know? I'm not a mind reader." You are not going to like my answer. You had better be a mind reader. Let me put it a better way. If that customer of yours is not glowing with loyalty, then you must assume that they fall within the statistics somewhere within your service practices. Maybe it is the way they have to schedule appointments, maybe it is the prearrangement process, maybe it is how long they have to wait for the phone to be answered, maybe it is the cost; the list could go on and on and on.

Now, here is the good news. The White House Council said that between 54 percent and 70 percent of unhappy customers will do business with us again if their complaint is served properly. That figure can jump to as high as 95 percent if it is served not only properly but also quickly. So, in essence we can come a long way down the road of turning a disgruntled customer into a loyal customer if we take their complaint seriously.

Here is something we need to focus on. Since 96 percent of unhappy customers won't tell you that they are upset, we have to jump for joy when we finally hear a complaint. Not that we are happy the challenge exists, but that we were told about it. Because once we know about the challenge, we can personally do something to solve it.

Let's talk about three types of difficult people and how we can best handle them. Before we get to that, though, the first thing I want you to understand is that it is not your job to change the difficult person. In fact, you can't. That is their job. Your job is to learn to handle them in the best possible way.

A number of years ago, I was at a banquet where the speaker was Dr. Mike Murdock. Knowing what I do for a living as a professional speaker and corporate trainer, and also knowing that I was pretty young and naïve at the time, Dr. Murdock decided to single me out in his speech. It made an impact on me that I will never forget. In front of all these people, Dr. Murdock said, "Mark, remember, you can't change anyone unless they want to be changed." Tough lesson! Right answer! The truth is that some of the difficult people in your life will always be difficult no matter what you do—because they choose to be difficult.

I also believe that it is important to put in place what I call a "Buffer Zone." A buffer zone is anything that will keep you calm for the first ten seconds of the encounter with the difficult person. You see, this is what happens. The difficult person says something nasty to you. The pressure inside of you begins to build as if your head is going to explode if you don't say something nasty back to them. You begin to get hot under the collar and your sweat glands begin to work overtime. You might be thinking, "Mark, I don't get a little hot under the collar, I have a blazing inferno under there." I understand. So, what do we do? We have to cap off the inferno. We have to smother the fire. If we don't do this, we may say or do something to the customer that we will regret as soon as it comes out of our mouths.

Again, a buffer zone is anything that will keep you calm for the first ten seconds. The first ten seconds are critical. Our emotions can be like a volcano ready to erupt and we have to slow down the volcano. Cool the emotion. Stay in control. Be proactive, not reactive.

Some of the most common buffer zones are counting to ten before you speak, taking a few deep breaths, or using an affirmation in your head such as "I am getting paid to serve this customer, I am getting paid to serve this customer, I am getting paid to serve this customer." As silly as those can be, especially that last one, they can be life savers in those difficult moments. Choose a buffer zone, either one of those or one you make up yourself. The point is that we all have to have a way to control our emotions in heated situations. When we do that, the rest of the situation is more manageable.

DIFFICULT CUSTOMER #1: THE NEGATIVE COMPLAINERS

They gripe, they whine, and nothing ever works out right—according to them. The negative customer is the one who always says it won't work. They are always looking at the down side and they are always complaining about something: the procedure, the weather, your price, their insurance, and they even complain about you. These are fun people to be around, aren't they? NOT!

How do we handle these people? First of all, don't let them get you down. Stay up and stay positive. The next time a difficult customer walks in the door, do three things. Handle them:

1. Politely

Always be polite. Always! Always! Always! Keep your buffer zone ready because you are going to need it. No matter what they say or do, follow your mom's advice. What did Mom always say? "Be nice, be kind, and be polite."

2. Positively

Counter their negative with a positive. If they say it won't work, ask them, "What if it *does* work? If we can get it to work, what benefit will that bring to your life?" Try to paint for them a picture of themselves benefiting from the positive outcome.

3. Firmly

Sometimes, you just have to be firm, as if you are dealing with a child. Remember, you can be firm and still be polite and positive. You are the expert. Say something like this, "Mr./Ms. Customer, I know you are uncomfortable and I know you doubt the outcome. I am asking you to trust me. My experience says for us to use this approach. If it doesn't work then we will reevaluate, but I believe it will work."

DIFFICULT CUSTOMER # 2: THE KNOW-IT-ALL

Have you ever been around a know-it-all? Isn't that fun? A know-it-all knows everything from apples to zoology and they want to share it all with you. The greatest challenge with a know-it-all is they will interrupt you a lot. This can be frustrating (which can lead to you saying something you shouldn't say or your tone sounding impatient) because they can soak up a lot of your valuable time.

What do you do when confronted with this type of customer? Can you ask a know-it-all not to interrupt you without irritating them? I think you can one time. Stay calm and say something like this, "I am glad you brought that up" (and you *are* glad because it shows interest). "I think when I get done explaining such and such it will make more sense. If not, please ask me at that time." If that doesn't work, then keep gently leading them back to the topic at hand.

One main thing to remember when dealing with know-it-alls is that they like you. They are not trying to be difficult. They are good customers who just have this quirk.

DIFFICULT CUSTOMER #3: THE HOSTILE

The hostile customer is the most difficult to deal with. They can be nasty, vulgar, and just plain mean. The main thing when dealing with a hostile is to let them vent. They don't even want to hear your apology or explanation until they have gotten it off their chest. Let them vent.

Another thing is that all this venom that they are spraying doesn't even have to do with you. Maybe they have had a bad day or a bad week and then something goes wrong when they are at your office. They fly off the handle and let you have it. You, unfortunately, are taking the heat for all the challenges in their life. That is not fair, but many times it is reality.

Another thing to remember is that you don't have to take abuse from a hostile customer. If they are getting vulgar, you can politely tell them that you don't allow that type of language in your office and if they continue they will be asked to leave.

The biggest challenge when dealing with hostile customers is that if anyone is going to go unstable on you, it is a hostile. If you sense this, or feel very uncomfortable, then don't handle this situation by yourself. Get help. Sometimes this will calm the situation or at least defuse it. Your safety and the safety of everyone else in the office is paramount. That takes precedence over making this type of customer happy.

Dealing with difficult customers is stressful and very frustrating. But when you take these action steps effectively and smoothly, it can be a very rewarding and profitable situation.

When handled properly, many times difficult customers turn into your most loyal customers.

Chapter Twenty

How to Give Bad News Without Stressing Out the Customer···or Yourself

HAVE YOU ever had to give bad news to a customer? It is very uncomfortable, isn't it? I have a statement you can memorize which is going to make those times somewhat easier. Here it is:

I'm sorry, Mr./Ms. Customer. We can't do that
because _____; however, we can do this_____.

Now, why does this work? Because it softens the blow. Many times, we use the word *policy* to explain to the customer why we can't do a certain thing. Let me tell you what happens when you use the word *policy*. Policy is a "hot" word. Certain words become hot words in our culture when they have been used over and over with a negative meaning behind them. *Policy* is such a word. Think about the last time you heard the word *policy*. It made you angry or at least frustrated, didn't it? It does the exact same thing to your customer. Another word that customers hate is the word *no*. They hate to be told something can't be done the way they want it done.

So, how do we tell the customer "no" or it is against our "policy" without using these words? You go right back up to our statement:

I'm sorry, Mr./Ms. Customer. We can't do that
because _____; however, we can do this_____.

When we apologize to the customer, they realize that we want to help. We aren't just blowing them off. Giving the explanation after the "because" tells them the same thing. It also gives the customer greater understanding of the situation. The statement after the "however" is huge because we aren't leaving the customer in no-man's-land. We have a solution for them, which is what they really want.

Every once in a while, you won't have a "however." Let's say that the reason you can't do what the customer requests is because it is against a government regulation. There is no "however." In this case, the customer might get a little testy with you but it is really toward the government, not you. They may take it out on you (the messenger) but the anger is really not pointed at you.

Using this little memorized statement does not mean that the customer is going jump up and down for joy and give you a big hug. Remember, it is still bad news that you are sharing with them. All this statement does is soften it to where it lessens the stress on them as well as on yourself.

Conclusion

Well, there you have it, my friend: *The 3 Pillars of Success for Funeral Directors.* A lot of common-sense ideas that can create great dividends for you and your funeral home. Common sense, yes. Common practice, no. I encourage you to take these ideas to heart and make the uncommon common for you. And before you know it...you will have the business of your dreams.

Thank you for investing in this book. My thoughts and prayers are with you. To your success.

God bless you,

Mark Bowser

About the Author

Mark Bowser

WHAT HE DOES: Mark teaches people and organizations how to win in Selling and Customer Service. Do you want to grow your sales? Maybe it is more appropriate to say that you *must* close more sales—and that you must close them now! Or, maybe you have a revolving door at your business entrance. Sure, customers are coming in—but then they leave, to never be seen again. You need repeat customers. Customers who are loyal. So whether you want to improve your results in closing more sales or creating loyal customers who sing your praises—Mark can help you do that!

HIS BACKGROUND: Mark has been a Professional Business Speaker since 1993. He has had the honor of presenting thousands of seminars and keynotes to help organizations and individuals reach the Selling and Customer Service Success they are looking for in this economy.

ORGANIZATIONS MARK HAS TRAINED INCLUDE:

Southwest Airlines
Princeton University
Purdue University
Ford Motor Company
Delta Faucet
Anderson University
Physicians Surgical Care
Sony Music
United States Air Force
Kutztown University
Herkimer County Community College
St. Luke's Methodist Church
FedEx Logistics
Dallas Public Schools
Kings Daughters Medical Center
United States Marine Corp
Office of the Inspector General, DOD

"I must say I've attended many seminars and workshops and by far this was the best. Mark was inspiring, knowledgeable, funny, and just a wonderful speaker. He held our attention for two days and then we wanted to hear more."

Charlene Cooke
Rutgers University Health Service

AUTHOR: Mark is the author of multiple books to help you succeed, including *Jesus, Take the Wheel*, *Sales Success*, *Nehemiah on Leadership*, and *Some Gave It All* with Danny Lane.

NEXT STEPS: If you would like to check Mark Bowser's speaking availability for your next event then please send him an email at info@markBowser.com. We also invite you to visit www.MarkBowser.com and register for our free Success Newsletters so that you can discover how you can sell more, serve customers passionately—and create customer loyalty.

More Books by Mark Bowser

Check them out at www.MarkBowser.com or www.Amazon.com/author/markbowser.

Sales Success
by Mark Bowser
(Contributions by Zig Ziglar, Tom Hopkins, and Scott McKain)

"Great Read! First of all, you can't argue with the 'A-list' contributing to this book. It reads well, is laid out nicely, and is easy to pick back up on during my hectic schedule interruptions.

"As a dentist, I am not a 'salesperson' and I do not force or try to talk patients into treatment. However, creating trust and value for a

product or service correlates to ANY profession. Learning how to create that value, present the issue/items, and communicate is key.

"Some patients want ideal health, some want beauty, some want it all. Some are realistic and some aren't. Unfortunately, a lot of healthcare workers cannot communicate findings, benefits or risks from treatment, or negatives from forgoing treatment well. As a result, there are a lot of untreated patients out there.

"As healthcare workers, it is good to hear feedback and views 'from the outside' (like a patient ourselves) so we know how to better our game, not talk over our fantastic patients, and in the end better our patients! This book helped me see views from a patient (i.e. non-dentist) perspective and the coaching from this rock-star team of contributors is spot-on.

"I highly recommend this book by Mark Bowser. Thanks for a great read!"

Jane Kirkpatrick

"I have been in sales for 20 years so as you can imagine I have read a lot of sales books. This book was by far my favorite! I normally approach a sales book as required reading but I found myself looking forward to each chapter!

Mr. Bowser expertly weaves great sales tips and best practices into a fictional story about a salesperson who in the beginning of the book is down on his luck and struggling with his sales. As the story progresses the main character learns a better way to be successful.

"I would recommend this book to all sales professionals and to non-sales people who enjoy a great story!"

Pamela

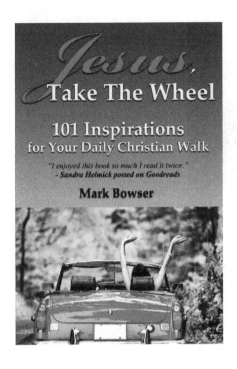

Jesus, Take the Wheel

Bible in a Year
(Mark Bowser wrote the monthly devotions)

Nehemiah on Leadership

Three Pillars of Success

Unlocking the Champion Within

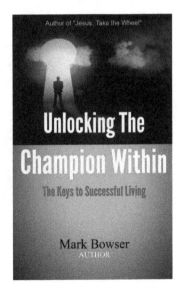

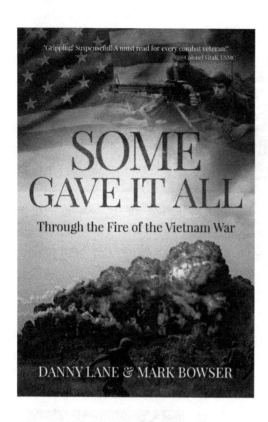

Some Gave It All
by Danny Lane and
Mark Bowser

"*Danny Lane and Mark Bowser have written an exciting roller coaster of an adventure. The amazing thing is that it is a true story.* Some Gave It All *grabbed me from the first paragraph and wouldn't let go until the last.*"

Pat Williams
Orlando Magic senior vice president
Author of *The Success Intersection*

"Some Gave It All *shows the horror of war and the emotional toll and recovery of a real American hero, Danny Lane. Without brave Marines like Danny Lane we would not be free. After reading this book, I will never forget that."*

Lee Cockerell, Executive Vice President (Retired and Inspired), Walt Disney World®Resort and best-selling author of *Creating Magic, The Customer Rule, Time Management Magic,* and *Career Magic*

"*This is an amazing story of courage and sacrifice. I'm almost at a loss for words. Every God-fearing American ought to read this. It'll get your heart pounding and you'll be forever grateful for the men and women who keep this country safe, including American hero Danny Lane. I am proud to have him on my staff as a combat tactics instructor."*

Jason Hanson, former CIA Officer and author of the New York Times Bestseller, *Spy Secrets that Can Save Your Life*; CEO of Spy Escape & Evasion Personal Protection Company

To get a Mark Bowser autographed copy of *Some Gave It All,* please go to www.MarkBowser.com/SomeGaveItAllBook.

Sample Catalog

For a complete listing of all our products, please visit
www.BrightCorporation.com
or call 1-800-428-6424 to request a physical catalog.

Have You Ever Thought About a Custom Designed Blanket?

If Not, You Should! Here's Why...

Imagine you have the privilege of listening in on a conversation that took place after your customer's service for their mom at your funeral home. What you hear touches your heart becasue you know you made a difference in a family's life. That is when you know you are on the right track when your funeral home makes a difference and a profit at the same time. Let's listen in to that possible conversation:

"It is hard to believe that it has been eight months since your mom passed away," said Georgia. "I am so sorry we were out of town during the service."

"I know you wanted to be here. I miss Mom every day, but I know she is at peace and full of joy. And, that gives me joy," said Jane as she and her best friend walked from the kitchen into the living room.

As they sat together on the couch sipping coffee, Georgia noticed a beautiful blanket hanging over the country rocking chair that held a prominent place in the room. "That is a beautiful blanket. The photographs are so clear. I love the arrangement and design of the photos of your mom and your family."

"That is my favorite piece in this room," said Jane as she got up and picked up the blanket to show her friend. "It helps me remember Mom and all the love she had for our family. Isn't it beautiful?"

"It is gorgeous. I love how the multiple pictures are balanced together. That is a wonderful memory keepsake. Where did you have that made?"

"ABC Funeral Home had is made for us. They treated us so kind during that time. I don't know how we would have gotten through all the details without their help. This blanket was a gift from ABC Funeral Home. When we arrived as a family for the visitation, they had it on display in the visitation room. You can imagine the feelings that it gave us when we walked in and saw it. I cried when I first saw it...Now, I come in here often and just look at it. Those photographs are the way I want to remember Mom. I give me comfort..."

"I can see why," said Georgia. "It is beautiful. I wish that the funeral home where we had my dad's service three years ago had done that."

"I am so grateful for ABC Funeral Home," said Jane. "They have been a blessing to our family."

That is the kind of conversation that comes from making a difference.

Custom Designed Blankets by Bright and Celebration Covers can create that difference. It can also help you build your business. Call Steve Bowser or John Sparacino today and they will share with you all the details so that you can create that difference too.

1-800-428-6424

Celebration Covers

Heirloom Montages

These frame-ready memorial keepsakes are a favorite among family members as a host of photos of their loved one's life are featured in a single visual storyline. From their earliest photo to the most recent, their stories unfold and become fresh reminders of a life well lived.

EASILY ACCOMMODATES UP TO 18 PHOTOS
FULL COLOR OR SEPIA FINISH MONTAGE
11 3/4" X 36"

Military Tribute Portraits

HONOR OUR VETERANS

Our Military Portraits memorialize a life of honor and service. We start with just your client portrait and add images from any branch of the military or public service. A fitting way to remember our veterans and public defenders and their service to our country.

Our custom designs are digital files ready to print or we can send directly to your local printer for same day pick up. Portraits are reasonably priced and we offer our 16" x 20" frames to easily drop in the printed image. Each portrait is as individual as the person!

STARTING AT
$30.00

QUALITY DARK WOOD & GOLD FRAMES WITH GLASS

For your convenience, we also offer 16" x 20" or 13" x 19" ready-made frames at wholesale pricing for you to pre-order and have on hand when you need them.

Frames always on hand & always ready!

NO. 556: GOLD & NO. 701: WALNUT
Set of 5.....$125
Set of 10.....$180

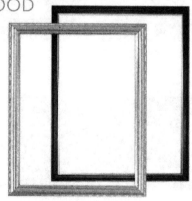

Custom Memorial Portraits

Memories really do become a somewhat magical part of healing the grief that is imparted when we lose someone we love. Families will cherish these custom portraits that reflect not only their loved one's image, but also favorite interest and passions representations as well.

Everyone loves a one-of-a-kind! Let us create that special memorial portrait that reflects the unique character of your family's loved one Give them something they'll never want to forget...a meaningful and celebratory keepsake.

HOW THE MAGIC BEGINS...

STEP 1 You email the image of your client's family member along with a list of up to four interests/passions suggestions.

STEP 2 Bright Corp.'s professional graphic designers design your custom 16" x 20" portrait for as little as $30 and forward the digital file to you or your designated printer via email.

STEP 3 Your local office supply retailer/printer can print the portrait for under $20 ...and there you have it!

MEMORIAL PORTRAITS

If your families would prefer a more traditional approach, our designers can also provide you with a simple one photo or two photo portrait.

Bright Corp

1-800-428-6424

info@brightcorporation.com
www.brightcorporation.com
P.O. Box 403
Anderson, IN 46015

MEMORIAL
PORTRAIT

MONTAGE OF MEMORIES
PORTRAIT

Canvas Wrapped Prints

HIGH QUALITY CANVAS PORTRAITS

POPULAR WITH CUSTOMERS!

TWO SIZES: 16" x 20" or 11" x 14"

We create our classic Montage

of Memories Portrait and have it wrapped and shipped or ready for a local printer pick-up!

Polaroid Montages

We have a new style of portraits great for sharing family memories. Featuring two extracted photos of the deceased and up to five family photos. Cherish these memories with your loved ones for a lifetime.

You can email us today to get started on your custom montage at info@brightcorporation.com

Window Frame Books

SPIRITUAL   **MILITARY**

MASCULINE

FEMININE   **PERSONALIZED**

OUR MOST VERSATILE BOOK
LOW OVERHEAD COST! TWO BOOKS...MANY LOOKS!

It's never been easy to meet all your client needs! One style can give you months of custom looks! any standard size memorial will slip right into the front window easily with transparent cover.

Tell us what insert you need and we will send it to you...*Free of Charge!* 1,000s of images to choose from!

We can print window inserts for your books with YOUR local scenery or landmarks! Email brightcorp@comcast.

NO. 96S: $9.95   **NO. 97S: $9.95**
Maroon Window Frame Register   White Window Frame Register Book
Book

Register Book Boxed Sets

ALL BOXED SETS
$33.95

2-UP FOLDERS
$36.95
PER 1000 (500 SHEETS)

8-1/2" x 11," Micro-Perfed, blank inside ready to print

REGISTER
BOOKS MAY
BE BOUGHT
SEPARATELY.
SEE PRICES
BELOW SET.

SINGLE FOLDERS
$35.65
PER 1000

8-1/2" x 5-1/2," flat, blank inside ready to print

NO. 26S: GOLD ROSE
Single Register Book
Reg. $14.85 **$12.95 each**
Box Set $33.95

NO. 12L: GOLD ROSE
4-1/4" x 5-1/2" Finished size
2up $36.95/m
Singles $35.65/m

NO. 276 GOLD ROSE
Reg. $67.50
Discount Price $63.65

NO. 33S: ROSE ARBOR
Single Register Book
Reg. $15.20 **$13.70 each**
Box Set $33.95

NO. 3632: ROSE ARBOR
4-1/4" x 5-1/2" Finished size
2up $36.95/m
Singles $35.65/m

NO. 363 ROSE ARBOR
Reg. $82.65
Discount Price $79.95

For a complete listing of all our products, please visit
www.BrightCorporation.com
or call 1-800-428-6424 to request a physical catalog.

NO. 27S: GOING HOME
Single Register Book
Reg. $15.60 **$14.15 each**
Box Set $33.95

NO. 2772: DOVE
4-1/4" x 5-1/2" Finished size
2up $36.95/m
Singles $35.65/m

NO. 277 DOVE
Reg. $84.75
Discount Price $79.95

NO. 34S: GARDEN PATH
Single Register Book
Reg. $15.20 **$13.70 each**
Box Set $33.95

NO. 3642: GARDEN PATH
4-1/4" x 5-1/2" Finished size
2up $36.95/m
Singles $35.65/m

NO. 364 GARDEN PATH
Reg. $84.75
Discount Price $79.95

FREE CUSTOMIZING
REGISTER BOOK
TEMPLATES

We have designed beautiful, matching register book opening pages so you can customize with ease! You just use our Word™ document template to customize anyof our standard designs. Easy to use and simple to print on your computer!

We want to help you add a personal touch for FREE!

NO. 79S: WHEAT
Single Register Book
Reg. $16.05 **$14.25 each**
Box Set $33.95

NO. 7122 WHEAT
4-1/4" x 5-1/2" Blank inside
2up $36.95/m
Singles $35.65/m

NO. 713 WHEAT
Reg. $70.65
Discount Price $66.60

NO. 46S: THE WAY HOME
Single Register Book
Reg. $15.55 **$14.05 each**
Box Set $33.95

NO. 4662: THE WAY HOME
4-1/4" x 5-1/2" Blank inside
2up $36.95/m
Singles $35.65/m

NO. 466 THE WAY HOME
Reg. $84.75
Discount Price $79.95

**NO. 40S:
REMEMBERING YOU**
Single Register Book
Reg. $15.65 **$14.30 each**
Box Set $33.95

**NO. 3702:
REMEMBERING YOU**
4-1/4" x 5-1/2" Blank inside
2up $36.95/m
Singles $35.65/m

NO. 370 REMEMBERING YOU
Reg. $84.75
Discount Price $79.95

NO. 65SAI: AZALEA (IVORY)
Single Register Book
Reg. $15.20 **$13.70 each**
Box Set $33.95

NO. 5882: AZALEAS
4-1/4" x 5-1/2" Blank inside
2up $36.95/m
Singles $35.65/m

NO. 588 AZALEAS
Reg. $70.65
Discount Price $66.60

For a complete listing of all our products, please visit
www.BrightCorporation.com
or call 1-800-428-6424 to request a physical catalog.

Memorial Folders

**NO. 3621:
CHAPEL
REFLECTIONS**
Blank inside

**NO. 3631:
ROSE ARBOR**
Blank inside

**NO. 3671:
CASCADING FALLS**
Blank inside

2-UP FOLDERS
$36.95
PER 1000 (500 SHEETS)
8-1/2" x 11," Micro-Perfed,
blank inside ready to print

SINGLE FOLDERS
$35.65
PER 1000
8-1/2" x 5-1/2," flat,
blank inside ready to print

Acknowledgements

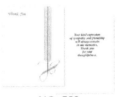

NO. 277 DOVE
$79.95 per 1,000

NO. 466 THE WAY HOME
$79.95 per 1,000

NO. 593
$67.30 per 1,000

Prayer Cards

NO. 223M

25-805: Creation

CPSIA information can be obtained
at www.ICGtesting.com
Printed in the USA
LVHW080954170720
660973LV00005B/530